THE ART OF
MASTERY

"Ralston provides both a real definition of mastery and a very detailed process to achieve it. The book highlights a path to mastery that applies to any chosen field. It provides specific principles and practices and points out potential pitfalls along the way. It is both encouraging and rigorous. There are no participation trophies in this book. One of its best features is guidance on how to benefit from the inevitable mistakes and failures along the path to mastering any activity. If you spend time and effort with this book, you will greatly benefit from the investment."

BOB NOHA, AIKIDO 6TH DAN AND CHIEF INSTRUCTOR
AT AIKIDO OF PETALUMA

"I so highly value the years I studied with Peter. In our work together, he immediately made me a better fighter and markedly so. Yet more importantly, he brought something else out: an internal energy, a state of being indescribable or undefinable, a power that I feel in every aspect of my life. He's not only a master in his art but a master teacher. That generous creative flow of universal light that he has allowed and brought forth in his own experience sets fire to everyone who studies with him."

RICHARD MOON, AIKIDO SENSEI/INSTRUCTOR 6TH DAN,
FACILITATOR IN INTERNATIONAL PEACE-BUILDING,
EXECUTIVE COACH, AND MEDIATOR

THE ART OF MASTERY

Principles of Effective Interaction

A Sacred Planet Book

PETER RALSTON

Park Street Press

Rochester, Vermont

Park Street Press
One Park Street
Rochester, Vermont 05767
www.ParkStPress.com

Text stock is SFI certified

Park Street Press is a division of Inner Traditions International

Sacred Planet Books are curated by Richard Grossinger, Inner Traditions editorial board member and cofounder and former publisher of North Atlantic Books. The Sacred Planet collection, published under the umbrella of the Inner Traditions family of imprints, includes works on the themes of consciousness, cosmology, alternative medicine, dreams, climate, permaculture, alchemy, shamanic studies, oracles, astrology, crystals, hyperobjects, locutions, and subtle bodies.

Cataloging-in-Publication Data for this title is available from the Library of Congress

ISBN 978-1-64411-643-2 (print)
ISBN 978-1-64411-644-9 (ebook)

Printed and bound in the United States by Lake Book Manufacturing, LLC
The text stock is SFI certified. The Sustainable Forestry Initiative® program promotes sustainable forest management.

10 9 8 7 6 5 4 3 2 1

Text design and layout by Kenleigh Manseau
This book was typeset in Garamond Premier Pro with Grand Gru and Nexa used as display typefaces

To send correspondence to the author of this book, mail a first-class letter to the author c/o Inner Traditions • Bear & Company, One Park Street, Rochester, VT 05767, and we will forward the communication, or contact the author directly at **PeterRalston.com**.

A Warrior is measured according to this:
That he learns from the dregs of the ancients and
extracts clear liquid from them.

CHOZAN SHISSAI,
EIGHTEENTH-CENTURY JAPANESE SWORDMASTER

Contents

On the Opportunity
of Mastery

In 1958 in Singapore I was asked by a Scottish friend of mine to join him in a Judo class. I had no idea what Judo was. But I started. Although I was only nine years old, it was the beginning of a long career that eventually lead me to mastering not only Judo but pretty much every traditional martial art as well. Then, and more importantly, I stepped beyond all traditional belief systems and worked hard to discover and master the existential nature of "fighting" itself. On the way, in 1978, I became the first non-Asian to win the full-contact World Tournament held in China—and I wasn't even a master then. I learned much more about mastery as life unfolded.

In addition to that pursuit, when I was about twenty, I became fascinated by Zen and the idea of enlightenment and so eventually dropped my medical studies at UCB and UCSF to pursue a different path. But just as I transcended traditional martial arts, after deeply studying the many "spiritual" and human growth practices, I eventually went beyond them and worked hard to pursue the Truth instead of any belief system. Through this commitment and focus, I managed to become personally and directly conscious of the nature of reality and the human condition. From these successes, I learned a great deal about the nature of mastery.

Although the principles of effective interaction are not in any way restricted to a particular endeavor, these two domains of mastery informed my insights:

1. A lifetime of mastering the fighting arts, and
2. A lifetime of investigating, contemplating, and facilitating consciousness pursuits—developing a deep experiential understanding of the human condition as a result.

The complementary nature of such disparate endeavors provided an unusual perspective that allowed me to discover overlooked principles and perceive uncommon realities that most often remain unseen when these domains are pursued individually.

Several decades ago I began wondering what skill was really all about. Due to my work in mastering the fighting arts combined with my contemplation and consciousness work, I realized that I was in the relatively unique position of perhaps being able to discover the nature of effective interaction and provide others with an opportunity to experience it for themselves. It turned out to be a very involved undertaking, leading to fascinating insights.

It demanded insight into and an experience of the components and makeup of skill as it applies to everyone as well as the discovery of possibilities and principles most people never experience. I will present these elements as this story unfolds. But keep in mind that for you to be effective, you will need to learn to generate simple experiences from what may seem like intellectually complex material.

To be clear, I'm not addressing how to improve an intimate partner relationship—after all, my background is in the fighting arts and I draw most of my knowledge about mastery from there. There are many principles and insights discussed here that certainly could be applied to partner relationships. But the focus of this book is on interactions that require skill where the people or objects you're interacting with are not necessarily aligned with your objectives. This is a broad arena. It is any activity you want to master where whatever it is you're interacting with is not doing it for you or with you, and may be working contrary to your goals—such activities as sports, business, arts of various kinds, combat, politics, and so on.

The purpose of this book is to empower you to create mastery in whatever field to which you want to devote yourself. Yet creating the ability that you seek will likely require a significant degree of personal transformation. To be sure, this communication is not about a few easy steps or pithy sayings that are supposed to improve your skill level in some way. It is for serious people who want to put energy, intention, and intelligence into mastering their field.

Obviously, mastery is about developing skill, but a study of it involves more than simply increasing effectiveness. The upcoming material provides a grounded investigation that can lead to a personal experience of the nature of effective interaction—so you can master your field—but it also provides an opportunity for deeper insights into yourself and life.

There are certain universal elements that I've discovered to be essential for creating mastery. I will address principles that apply to any field, and also specific requirements necessary in practices involving physical as well as nonphysical skills. Although I may tend to present too much material, I would feel remiss if I didn't provide it for you. The details may be difficult to understand or easily incorporate and you may have to struggle to make it real for yourself, but such undertakings are part of any learning endeavor.

The experiences shared in each section of the book are real and attainable—I know because I have experienced and used everything in this book. I am sure that using them will also help you increase your access to mastery. Yet much of the material will seem abstract at first, and there is a danger of assuming intellectual understanding is all that can be had. That is not an assumption you can afford in this endeavor.

Once you understand what is being said, and have applied it to your own field, if you don't have an experience that is different from your previous experience, your skill level will obviously remain unchanged. On the other hand, if you do the work to turn everything in here into a new, deep, and real functional experience, you can attain mastery.

You'll have to be patient though, because quite a bit of groundwork has to be laid before we can effectively address the powerful principles and actions that will ultimately make the greatest difference. So, if something is being addressed that seems unrelated to getting on with the job of mastery, remember, it may well make sense—or may be needed in order to lay the groundwork for something—later on.

Pursuing mastery needs to be done from the ground up so that our foundations are solid and can support such a transformative endeavor. To grasp all that is said will be difficult, and training will be time consuming. Yet the communications in this book hold the keys that can open many doors leading to genuine mastery.

Just the pursuit of mastery alone leads to an improvement in life and self-esteem. Its pursuit should be a satisfying activity that provides profound experiences as well as joyful moments. To be sure, there will likely be a lot of hard work accompanied by failure after failure, but the quest itself nourishes you through the hard times, and the rewards that accumulate over time should keep you going. I recommend you adopt a disposition that makes it a fun and exciting adventure.

To become a master at any skill, it takes the total effort of
your heart, mind, and soul working together in tandem.
MAURICE YOUNG

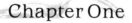

Chapter One

Committing to the Pursuit of Mastery

It's Up to You

The secret to mastery is to know how to take appropriate action in relation to what's occurring to produce desired results. Even though we try to do this all the time, it doesn't always work out. That's because there's a catch. What we don't notice is that what we experience doesn't match what's occurring, or what's there, and that our perceptive-awareness doesn't have all the elements necessary to act appropriately. This can change.

If you are looking for an easy five-step plan to mastery, however, this isn't that. It is a comprehensive and thorough look into what it takes to actually achieve mastery. Most people don't do that; that's why it's rare.

> *If people knew how hard I had to work to gain my mastery,*
> *it would not seem so wonderful at all.*
>
> MICHELANGELO

The pursuit of mastery is not an easy road. You are likely to be overwhelmed by the sheer volume of ideas to come as you try to intellectually follow and understand them all. There is much to know and to personally experience. But if you don't think it's possible for you personally, you're not likely to pursue it.

You might think it takes too much work or you don't have the time or energy to put in. Besides, why go to all the trouble? What does it get you? Since what it gets you is really unknown, you may not even have the motivation to undertake such a task. Yet even if you leap past such obvious hurdles and commit to pursuing mastery, it still does take a lot of work. The truth is, however, that other humans have become masters, and so the only requisite is to be human—if one of us can do it, then it's possible for all of us. So, be clear: the decision isn't if you can, but if you're willing.

Over the years, while trying to convey what it takes to attain mastery, I found that my communications were far too complex and involved for most people to grasp. Indeed, latching onto and putting into action just a few of the principles expressed here does make a difference. But real mastery requires more.

Mastery is about being unusually skillful in your field. It may take commitment and work, but such a pursuit is life-changing even before any attainment. It provides a new and powerful experience rarely achieved. Committing to mastery transforms life into a deep adventure, increases your self-esteem, and not only gives you a reason to get out of bed in the morning but also provides you with a sense of being an exceptional person aiming for heights rarely attained. Simply, the pursuit of mastery takes you into another world, one of wonder and discovery.

The difference between a student and a master is, the master has failed more times than the student has tried.

MAC DUKE

Changing Your Mind

A significant part of your experience you call your mind—that inner activity where you think and feel, imagine and calculate, remember and plan. It is also where you believe and assume, have been programmed and educated, developed characteristics and patterns of behavior, and formed your self-concept and self-esteem. Mind is what dictates actions and reactions, states and moods. It calculates possibilities and creates strategies. It generates doubts and convictions. There is no part of your experience that isn't at least influenced by your mind. Do you think this place, where you experience so much, might have something to do with your skills and abilities? Absolutely!

It is essential that you put yourself in the driver's seat of your pursuit and efforts. No one else can do it for you—only you can. Therefore, mastery demands responsibility. It is something that must take place in your own mind and body. Obviously, it isn't going to happen if you don't do it, and you can't do it unless you genuinely experience what it takes to do so. One of the central demands for mastery is to be able to change your mind.

To attain mastery, you're required to change your thinking, perceptive-experience, and actions. All these activities occur as functions of your mind. Clearly, mental activities are of the mind, but even a physical action doesn't occur unless it is generated by your brain. If you can't change what occurs in your mind, and thus your experience, you can't become masterful. One of the first changes you need is an openness beyond how you presently think of and relate to the matter of mastery.

Mastery, or skill of any kind, is about relationship. It is determined by how you *relate* with another, an object, or some activity. Sometimes, without thinking, you might view mastery as a subjective or solo affair, since it is clear that you are the one who must create it. At first blush it could appear how you relate to or experience others or objects is irrelevant. But this is not a view you can afford.

When we think about it, we see skill can only occur in relationship. The way we relate to another, or to movement, a ball, an instrument, or to whatever—that is the only place where mastery can show up. Although we are responsible for creating our relating, it is how we experience and interact with the not-self that determines our level of skill.

We have all heard the phrase "mind over matter." Although, when push comes to shove, most of us don't seem to really believe it, we must admit that if our experience determines our level of skill then being able to change our mind is crucial to our pursuit. We'll see that understanding how the mind works—so we can learn how to control and change it—is essential for mastery.

One of the reasons we need to be able to change our minds and our experience is that it is not only possible, but likely, that what's occurring—what's really there—is different from our experience of it. This might be a hard thing for us to grasp, because we assume our perceptions and interpretations reflect exactly what's there. But this just isn't so.

We will learn that our experience has many subjective influences that bend and twist it in ways both subtle and gross that interfere with accurately reflecting what's occurring. Given this condition, work must be done to change our perceptive-experience to more precisely reflect whatever we're interacting with—as it *is*. This provides us with powers and abilities we wouldn't have otherwise.

Beyond changing the mind, we must also learn to control it. I can't tell you how many times I've said to my apprentices "control your mind." Without a certain mastery of mind, mastering anything else isn't going to happen.

To be clear, I am not inviting you to make this into an ideal of perfection. We are talking about mastering a field, not all of reality or even all of mind. Many masters who are incredible at controlling their minds in their fields may not control it in their personal lives or in other endeavors. But in mastering your endeavor, mind control is essential.

One of the core skills of mind control is to be able to let go. We all have habits and beliefs, ways of doing things, and overlooked assumptions that get in the way of progressing beyond our current level of skill. We have to be able to let these go. Once we can get our experience to be accurate, drop detrimental habits and beliefs, and recognize and eliminate ineffective assumptions, we are empowered to relate far more skillfully.

> *Truly creative people in all fields can temporarily suspend their ego and simply experience what they are seeing, without the need to assert a judgment. They are more than ready to find their most cherished opinions contradicted by reality.*
>
> ROBERT GREENE

Furthermore, we must increase our awareness and sensitivity because we need access to more information than a sluggish or cloudy awareness can provide. Toward that end, finding a way to make whatever we are attempting more effortlessly achieved forces us to search in places we wouldn't otherwise as well as to discover finer distinctions and overlooked principles that make such effortlessness possible—thus heightening our awareness and moving us closer to mastery.

This deepening awareness partners with a growing body of experiential knowledge that provides a tremendous amount of information about each moment we are in. I will be introducing many distinctions that will expand your perceptive-experience so you can access far more information than normal. I will also present operating principles that can make a huge difference in your abilities. Some principles are essential for mastery and these must be deeply understood and adopted. When that is done, mastery is almost inevitable.

You currently experience some level of skill in your field. You may experience a degree of competence, or you may experience being inept or challenged. Whatever you experience now is the starting point. The trick is to change this very experience.

In the old days, I would allow students into my "boxing" class only twice a year. When the new people came in I would tell them two things. First, "90 percent of boxing is mind—the physical component is relatively simple, and although improvement needs to constantly continue, everything else occurs through the use of your mind." I would also tell them, "Whatever you experience now has to change, because you don't experience yourself as a master boxer." These statements indicate an essential principle for mastery: your mind, experience, and yourself must change. This holds true no matter the field.

> *A man cannot understand the art he is studying if he only looks for the end result without taking the time to delve deeply into the reasoning of the study.*
>
> MIYAMOTO MUSASHI

Taking It On

In the end, you will have to make all of this yours. You must become the authority in the matter. It is the only way to master anything.

To be able to translate the overwhelming amount of detail to come—and what will at first probably seem like rather abstract or disconnected communications—into real growth and improvement, you will have to ground it in your experience and actions. As each point is made, it is best to take it into your field and work with it there. Observe it in action. Then it will become less of an abstract idea and more of an observable experience.

I will describe a great deal. But remember, a description of something isn't the thing itself. An explanation of how something works doesn't make something work—only making it work does that. A description has to become an experience that is taken to action for it to make a difference. Toward that end, beyond just hearing a description, you really need to experience each section and each distinction or principle in operation. The description itself doesn't do that.

For example, if you pick up a rock and hold it in your hand, this is a real, albeit simple, experience. Quickly, you know much about the rock and you can describe it in detail. You can talk about its gray-brown color and its odd, uneven shape. You might describe the feeling of smooth rounded lumps on one side, and the rough texture of the mostly flat other side, as well as the warmth it absorbed from sitting in the sun. You have all this information simply by holding and gazing at the rock.

But if I don't share your experience of this rock, and perhaps have never even seen a rock before, your description might well leave me out in the cold. I won't have what you have unless I can somehow translate all those descriptions into one simple experience. Here, I won't be describing rocks, I will be speaking about you and your experience and actions. But just like having a rock in your hand, you must turn all this talk into something solid and real for yourself.

Mastery will take a lot of work, so at some point you need to decide if you want to do the work or not. Obviously, that's up to you. You could just get an impression or find a few things that seem to improve your skill level. But if you want to experience everything I'm going to present, roll up your sleeves.

I know it is possible for you do that, because I have experienced and used everything in this book—that's why it's here. But my attempt to communicate it or explain it is different than the experience that makes those attempts possible. Please, don't let my inability to make the communication more easily accessible stop you from grasping it.

We would imagine that if Mozart, a master of his art, were to try to communicate what he knew and how he did what he did to someone just learning music, the student would have a hard time understanding or experiencing what was being conveyed. Work would have to be done and leaps in listening and learning undertaken. I'm not trying to imply I'm in such rarified company. What I am doing is inviting you to soberly assess what it might take to experience all that is to come.

Again, much of what will be said may seem abstract unless you can ground it in something real for yourself. I can't overemphasize that you use your field of mastery—and if you don't have one, choose something you can use—and apply what's said to that. Find a way to ground each point in your field and your experience, or at least realistically imagine how each point applies to specifics in your field.

Now, on to the work.

> *Mastery is not a function of genius or talent. It is a function of time and intense focus applied to a particular field of knowledge.*
>
> ROBERT GREENE

Chapter Two
Mastery—
The Short Version
A Brief Overview

As I've said, incorporating the amount and complexity of the material in this book could be overwhelming. It can be difficult to grasp let alone remember and apply. Therefore, I want to first present the whole book in an extremely reduced form, just touching on the main points you're going to encounter. Perhaps you will grasp it all in its short form quickly and save yourself a lot of time and effort. At least I hope it sets the stage, creating an introduction to as well as an openness and preparedness for the more complex communications to come.

With this overview, you might better understand a more detailed description when you encounter it and be able to view it within the context of the whole. Being exposed to and getting a sense of each point allows you to contemplate and consider it before having to tackle a flood of information about it. I suggest you dwell on each of the major points for a bit, even in this short form, and apply it in your field as best you can to get some experience of its reality before going to the next point. In this way, you develop an experience that relates to what's being communicated prior to delving more deeply into the details, thus giving you a stronger foundation from which to further pursue the material.

A. On the Nature of Mastery

What Is Mastery?

Mastery is about being able to reproduce results nonrandomly and consistently. You need to ground your idea of mastery—getting past unrealistic fantasies—but still demand an uncommon level of skill. Mastery should be the zenith of your endeavor.

Why Should You Pursue Mastery?

Simply pursuing mastery changes and improves your life—creating a deeper satisfaction in your living and much higher self-esteem—even before any attainment. After attainment, it provides a new and powerful experience rarely achieved.

Practice, Principle, Being

In pursing mastery, there are three stages useful to embrace: practice, principle, and being.

Practice involves lots of repetition. With practice, you begin to become privy to the principle(s) behind how some activity works. Consciously searching out an experience of these principles increases the likelihood you'll find them.

Let's look at traditional definitions of "principle" that may apply.

- a fundamental truth that serves as the foundation for a system of behavior or for a chain of reasoning
- a rule governing one's personal behavior
- a natural law forming the basis for the construction or working of a machine
- a fundamental source or basis of something
- a fundamental quality or attribute determining the nature of something; an essence

Here, a principle is what dominates your experience and actions so that these unfold in a particular way. When an effective principle governs your actions, success is almost inevitable. You need to discover, experience, and then surrender to whichever principles are required to be effective in the endeavor you are trying to master.

Surrendering to a principle means you make the principle dominant over your internal state and actions. Once this is the case, you will be effective in any activity that is based upon or relates to that principle; it will allow you to perform feats most people can't.

If you want a principle to be an aspect of your life, you can adopt it as a feature of your character. This is *living as* or *being* the principle.

Knowledge Useful for Mastery: Foundation Principles

First, **responsibility** puts you in the position where you are at the source of your thinking, actions, and learning, without which you can't master a thing.

Second, the fact that **your actions are always related to your perceptive-experience** means that *how* you experience things will determine your effectiveness.

Third, your experience and what is occurring aren't necessarily the same thing, and in order to be effective **you must relate to what's actually occurring.**

How We Assess Ability

Skill is a function of a self and whatever that self is relating to—an object, an event, or another. You assess what you can or can't do by comparing what's encountered to your knowledge and assumptions about yourself. Getting free of dysfunctional assumptions about yourself helps open a door to mastery.

The Possibility of Changing Your Experience

You need the ability to experience what's objectively there for you and not what's subjectively added. Much of your assessment of your capabilities is quite subjective and built upon many assumptions, and you judge yourself accordingly. In this pursuit, the effort of trying to manage or suppress what's judged isn't an effective use of your time. You must move from judging and managing your subjective assumptions to a more open and objective experience of what's possible.

How We Relate to Process

Everything you do is a process. Because your automatic focus is on managing circumstance, your attention often locks onto trying to attain results in a less than effective way. Results are always part of a process. When it comes to your volitional actions, a result is simply the part of a process that you engaged that process to achieve. Attending to the process throughout, rather than fixating on the goal, produces a better result.

Often, when you encounter a problem, your attention contracts into the place the problem is encountered. When you step back and look at the whole process, you can see where the process went off-track and so are empowered to make a correction and get back on track.

The finer and more accurate the distinctions you make in the processes involved in any endeavor you might undertake, the greater your mastery will be.

B. The Principle of Effective Interaction

The Principle of Effective Interaction

Your actions must relate appropriately to the occurring event, so that the purpose for the interaction is realized.

Notice the difference between the principle that currently governs your actions—that *your actions are related to your experience*—and the principle of effective interaction. Your experience includes layers that are not what *is* but interpretations of "has been," "will be," or "should be," as well as many biased or reactive mental and emotional additions that aren't what's occurring except in your own mind.

Once experiencing what's there for itself, your actions need to be appropriate for realizing your objectives in relation to this event.

Dissecting the Principle of Effective Interaction
Your Actions

"Action" is what you do—physically and mentally. Adjustments to your actions should take into account everything you do; they should not just focus on one isolated aspect.

Must Relate

"Relate" means: "make a connection between." Your actions need to connect with and respond to whatever it is you are interacting with. One of the principles that greatly assists responsive and appropriate relating is to "follow" what's happening—to perceive and have your actions relate to everything that is occurring as it is occurring.

Appropriately

The purpose and objectives for an interaction determine what is appropriate, and so those need to dictate your actions. If your actions are in the process of realizing your objective, they are appropriate; if not, they are not. Of course, the trick is to know beforehand whether or not an action is going to be effective, ergo appropriate. By comparing each moment of circumstance to your objective, you can assess what actions you need to take to realize that objective.

To the Occurring Event

What normally occurs is an automatic, habitual, and massive application of personal interpretation and bias to anything perceived. If you are acting in relationship to something that is not actually the occurring circumstance you will not be effective. You need the ability to see what is actually there and relate it to your objectives, *not* to yourself.

Tailor Your Actions to Your Objective

A finely tuned sensitivity should arise from an ongoing comparison of the arising process to your objective. Strategies can then be created to achieve your objective. Strategies and goals should exist solely to *serve* the objective. Never make the strategy the objective.

C. Transforming Your Perceptive-Experience

Making Distinctions

"Distinction" refers to anything that is experienced or perceived—an object, a thought, an image, a relationship, a dimension, numbers, words, ideas, a feeling, emotion. Everything experienced in any way or on any level constitutes a distinction. (For more on distinction see my books: *The Book of Not Knowing,* chapter 24, section: "The Distinction 'Distinction'"; and *The Genius of Being,* chapter 3, section: "What Is a Distinction?")

To accomplish mastery, you must make every distinction needed to do that job. When it comes to distinctions you already make, your job is to refine and become more sensitive or sophisticated within that experience. When it comes to distinctions you haven't made that are required for mastery in your field, you'll have to create them. Two domains of distinctions are "objective" and "non-objective."

Objective Distinctions

"Objective" here refers to the world of objects. To master any physical activity, you need to attend to and increase your sensitivity of the foundational elements of the physical world. You also need to become fully conscious of your own body. Alignment with the body's design maximizes physical ability. (For much more detail about the effortlessly effective use of the body, see my book *Zen Body-Being*.)

Whatever the body is interacting with—gravity, space, a ball, an instrument, another person, a paint brush, or something else—demands making sophisticated distinctions relative to that object and adhering to pertinent principles regarding interacting with that object. In any physically based endeavor, every one of the objective distinctions needs to become part of your feeling-experience. In primarily non-objective fields, you can often apply these distinctions metaphorically.

Objective Qualities: Keep a feeling-connection with the weight, shape, design, and substance of any object.

Space: Stay immersed in three-dimensional awareness, and constantly feel changes in spatial relations.

Process: Know the potential and possibilities in each stage of an occurring process, and relate appropriately. Don't focus on the result; treat it for what it is: part of the process.

Force: Fully acknowledge the presence, amount, kind, and intent of incoming forces; manage, utilize, or neutralize these forces; and stay balanced and unified so as to maximize applying force.

Timing: Know when to act and when to wait.

Non-Objective Distinctions

The non-objective realm of your experience includes such intangible aspects as thinking, feeling, and perception. Knowing how your mind works in these largely overlooked and automatic processes allows you to change your experience when necessary.

Seven Non-Objective Components
Perception

The "perception" of the interaction is the basis from which an interaction is known at all. Perception alone, however, doesn't provide all of the information necessary to take appropriate action. For that you need interpretation. Be open to discovering something overlooked or unseen, including errors in your perceptions and assessments. This empowers you to more fully grasp what is arising in each moment.

⁓

Creatively question your perceptions, and stay
open to what may be unnoticed.

⁓

Interpretation

"Interpretation" is the automatic and speedy mental activity of categorizing and "knowing" what things are. Interpretation gives you necessary information about what is happening. But much of what you mistake for interpretation is a bias born from your own desires, fears, and projections and is influenced by your beliefs and assumptions. To be effective, your interpretations need to relate whatever you are interacting with to your current objectives and the purpose for the interaction, not to your personal needs.

⁓

Interpretation should accurately represent
what's there, and not be weighed down with
personal stuff.

⁓

State

"State" is the particular condition of mind that someone is in at any given time. It seems as if your mood, emotions, and state of mind are produced by circumstances. But this is only because your interpretation automatically relates circumstances to yourself and you react accordingly, making it appear like you really have no choice in the matter. Yet your state of mind is something you are generating; it doesn't have to be circumstantially derived. You need the ability to quickly change your state when appropriate. For example, becoming calm, present, and fully aware is often a useful state. Adopting an appropriate state will likely be your most valuable asset for mastery.

⌇

*Master your state of mind and create the best
state for the job at hand.*

⌇

Extrapolation

"Extrapolation" is having a concept of what will occur in the future drawn from the patterns seen in what has occurred so far. When you fixate on an extrapolation, holding it as an occurring fact rather than a concept of the future, you tend to miss any changes that occur in the activity until it's too late to relate to them appropriately.

⌇

Keep all extrapolation up to date.

⌇

Strategy

The plan or "strategy" you choose to reach an objective has perhaps the greatest impact on your success or lack of it. The "what to do," once you have accurate data and an appropriate state, is what decides whether or not mastery takes place.

"Purpose" is why you take something on, the "field" is the activity you use to pursue your purpose, and the "objective" is your strategic goal.

You should immediately compare your objective to what's occurring; this provides an idea of what needs to occur to reach your goals. It is imperative that you do not make the objective subservient to the strategy.

You are also likely to have hidden personal objectives that influence your interpretations, strategy, and actions. These will make you ineffective and you'll not know why. Being clear about the objective and purpose for an interaction is the first step toward avoiding this mistake.

The task here is to clearly discern your objectives and not let personal goals influence your strategies.

~

Never make the strategy master over the objective. The strategy should always serve the objective, and change the moment it doesn't.

~

Impulse

Once a strategy is in place, you will make a decision about what action to take. From this decision arises an intent, and this intent immediately takes the form of an "impulse" that produces an action. All of this can seemingly take place at light speed. The feeling-distinction of impulse is the activity that creates action. It links your *intention* to *action*.

It's important to distinguish between an impulse that is on purpose and all the other impulses that arise as reactions to a self-referencing personal agenda. When you are trying to have your individual or personal needs or desires met, you are in the wrong frame of mind for effectively interacting with others or objects that have nothing to do with your personal agenda. For mastery, you need to generate effective impulses that are free of personal reactivity and drives.

~

Wed all impulses to the current event, and allow your impulses to be creative.

~

Interpretation of the Other's Non-Objective Components

In any endeavor involving others, this is one of the most important distinctions to make. It's actually a conglomerate of distinctions. You need to be constantly aware of what the other person or people are experiencing.

Another's experience will not be the same as yours and may be founded on a different framework of mind and a different value system. Because most people don't put enough attention on a clear and unbiased experience of what's so for the other, they are short-changed in their ability to interact effectively.

Action follows intent. When the intent changes, so does the action.

Watch the water, not the fish.

• • •

See the road they are on
and you will know which way
they must turn.

If you see that to which the other is bound, you will know what actions they will take.

～

Develop a refined and accurate feeling-sense of
the other's experience in each moment.

～

All of the objective and non-objective distinctions mentioned above already occur in some form for everyone, yet they are usually all mushed together in an experience that is simplistic and insensitive as well as mixed with personal agendas that don't serve the individual or actually get in the way. Your job is to clarify and refine these distinctions.

Feeling Translation

Once each distinction is individually studied and experienced, they all need to be put together—translated, if you will—and act as a whole in one sophisticated but simple feeling-experience that includes all of the distinctions needed for mastery in your field. This feeling-experience will be able to quickly and effectively relate all incoming data to your objectives and your current strategy.

Reaction Versus Response

So that we are on the same page about action springing from a feeling-sense, it is important to understand the difference between response and reaction. A response arises from a calm mind and sensitive awareness. The intent of responsive action is to produce what is needed and appropriate. A reaction arises from automatic impulses that tend to be motivated by such activities as fear, desire, resistance, vulnerability, anger, or other knee-jerk self-protective actions. Reactions are an attempt to solve or end the apparent source of danger or dilemma. Mastery requires appropriate response, not reactivity.

Rethinking Relationship

Mastery is all about relationship—you relating with something or someone else. To help rethink overlooked assumptions that govern the general cultural interpretations of relationship, here are four assertions and a recommendation:

> Relationship is not an object (it is an assessment and an activity).
>
> Relationship cannot "not work." It is only what is occurring between two or more.
>
> Mastery is not personal, nor do you have any "choice" in the matter.
>
> Interaction is strictly relative; limitation and possibility co-exist.
>
> Discover and eliminate all ineffective assumptions and beliefs.

Rethinking Learning
New Ways of Learning

I encourage people not to stop at the first conclusion they discover about why some activity works or doesn't work but to stay open and continue to investigate. From this practice, you are empowered to learn more quickly and encounter new ideas, dynamics, or experiences that aren't restricted to past patterns. As well, you may eliminate overlooked assumptions that have influenced your original conclusion.

People hearing and perceiving everything within their current thinking and beliefs is a major obstacle to learning. Radical experimentation and experiential inquiry serve as doorways to break through this obstacle. In this way, you "put your ass on the line" to produce breakthroughs in your current experience and modes of thinking, feeling, and acting.

Powerful Learning

People stand on their own personal experience as the arbiter of what to receive and what to reject about anything communicated. This creates a severe limitation on one's ability to learn. I recommend that a more effective way to learn from someone—a respected teacher or master—is to, in a sense, "become" the other person, taking on the other's experience wholesale and without filter. If you grasp or experience what the other person is experiencing, you can do or understand whatever it is they can do and understand. Such an approach can cut the learning time down tremendously.

If you're breaking new ground that no one has mastered heretofore, you'll have to create new experiences from which to do it on your own.

D. Principles and States That Empower Mastery

Just as various fields use the principles found in Sun Tzu's *Art of War,* you must translate the upcoming principles into forms appropriate to your field of interaction.

You need to be able to apply any learned principles to your entire field and, to really understand it, to other fields as well. Unless you experientially understand the principle itself, not just the description or method used to invite you to get it, mastery will remain elusive.

A Couple of Actions Useful for Effective Interaction
Align to the Principles of an Effortlessly Effective Body

Sensitive and complete body-awareness increases the possibilities and effectiveness in any physical interaction. (See my book *Zen Body-Being*.)

Practice Creating Alternative Strategies

It is a valuable practice to ascertain many possible paths to accomplish your objective. If at any moment your approach is not working, you can seamlessly change, switching to another path. This practice also expands your mental prowess for creating strategies.

A Few Essential Principles
Don't Ignore

Include all occurring factors, including those that might otherwise be unattended.

The Effortless Principle

The principle of searching for the most effortless approach to accomplish your results forces you to look in directions you wouldn't have looked in otherwise. Instead of achieving effortlessness after mastering something, consider using the effortless principle to help you master it.

Mind-Body Alignment Principle

A very important principle for any physical activity that definitely improves your level of effectiveness and power is the mind-body alignment principle. When the mind moves ahead of the process as it's occurring, a split will happen between mind and body and your actions will relate to a future projection—*not* to the occurring process. This weakens the process a great deal. In every segment of a process the mind should be fused with and doing only that moment of the process.

The Power of Correction

Correction is changing whatever is not effective into what is. The more sensitive you are to what must occur in order to realize an objective, and *when* it must occur, the sooner you will know whether the process is going to work out or not. When the process is going off-track you will need to change your strategy and actions, and probably your thinking or attitude.

Although a certain amount of relating to an extrapolation may well be appropriate, you must always bear in mind that changes are to be expected and not depend on "jumping to a conclusion" as if it is a reality. Instead, stay with the process and make corrections as you go.

Elements of Correction

Not Knowing: create a blank state from which to change course as necessary.

Freedom from Assumptions: discover and discard inappropriate assumptions.

Letting Go: give up whatever you are doing that is ineffective.

Generating: create new thought, strategy, and/or action that is effective.

The Need to Internalize

You won't be able to be effective with all this if it remains mere hearsay or learned abstractions. The actions you take must be based on an *experience* that already internalizes all of these disparate parts.

Creative Intelligence

However you accomplish it—through study and consideration, experience and wisdom, questioning and investigation, or contemplation and insight—some form of creative intelligence is a must. It is the final ingredient when all of the other ingredients have been accounted for.

This kind of intelligence must operate outside of fear and ambition and without attachment to winning or losing, creating a conglomerate experience that is highly sophisticated and tailored to each particular circumstance. From this experiential state, the "how" of it becomes obvious as you relate your objective to what's there. If not, "fast problem solving" is undertaken.

E. Powerful Operating Principles for Mastery

So, again, how can you bring all of the components of effective interaction together? You must find principles that do just that. It might be useful to review again the nature of a principle in the section "Practice, Principle, Being" (p. 14) before going on to the next section.

Laying a Foundation

The task of taking all of this information into action is considerable. To do that, you need to understand the principles and states that make it possible. After you've managed to improve the operations of your own body and mind, turn your attention to principles that improve your level of skill.

Before addressing powerful interactive operating principles, it is useful to master these foundational principles:

Listening: Knowing what's there.
Outreaching: Connecting with what's there.
Yielding: Neutralizing or managing what's there when needed.

Powerful Interactive Operating Principles

There are several principles that are worth gold when it comes to pursuing mastery in an interactive field. Adhering to any one of these principles ensures that your actions are completely designed by the actions and intent of the other(s) involved or the activity that is occurring.

Following: stick to the activity like glue.

Joining: merge with and contribute to the activity to take it over.

Complementing: shape your actions around arising activity in an advantageous way.

Leading: offer what is desired to draw another's actions and take control of them.

Cutting: reduce the potential for disruptive action to take shape; and don't fall behind.

Sprouting: nip all unwanted activity in the bud by destroying it at its origin.

Borrowing: absorb incoming forces and cycle them back to the source.

Choiceless: in each moment take actions that can't be thwarted.

Changing: allow no effective strategy to be formed against you.

A World of Operating Principles

As you move through these principles you will start to glean a few threads that connect them all. They all put you in a very sophisticated and responsive relationship to what's occurring. From there, mastery is a small step to take.

I recommend that after you have worked with all of the points made in this short version and have played with them as best you can to get some experience with them, then go on to the detailed version.

MASTERY

The Principles of Skill and Effective Interaction

The Long Version

Patience, my friend. Once again, I say, Patience. In an era "plagued" with speed, doggedness of character and drudgery of persistence is the only guarantee to mastery.

UFUOMA APOKI

Chapter Three
On the Nature of Mastery

WHAT IS MASTERY?

Many of us like movies of superheroes and ultra-skilled people. We are fascinated by the possibility of magical powers being given to one of us mortals who then turns these powers into successfully managing difficult circumstances and helping the weak. If not mysterious magical powers, we are still fascinated by a normal person like one of us finding a way to become an exceptional superhero by developing unbelievable skills. We might love these fantasies and wish we had such abilities, but most of us either don't think it is possible or aren't willing to devote the time and energy to make it happen.

Obviously, the idea of mastery can vary, and although the myths and fantasies that accompany it might provide inspiration, they overlook the reality of the work involved. Mastery always relates to being very effective at some activity. The basic idea of mastery revolves around being able to reproduce results nonrandomly and consistently. Within your field, when you can consistently produce the results you want, you'll consider yourself effective. But when do you become masterful?

First, perhaps, we should bring down to earth a couple myths that tend to be attached to the idea of mastery. Often mastery is held as an ideal of extraordinary perfection, the ability to do magical things without the possibility of failure. When we think masters walk on water and are invulnerable in their field, it is useful to remember that every master that ever lived has experienced failure in their lives. They are human like everyone else. Also, sometimes we think masters know everything and can do anything. But the truth is, masters most frequently master only one field of activity and don't have any extraordinary ability in any other field, and they certainly don't know everything. Such ideals make the goal of mastery seem inaccessible to mortals like us.

A story I like to share comes from a friend of mine, Robert, who studied with the founder of Aikido, Ueshiba, and traveled with him to teach around Japan. At one point, he heard that Ueshiba had tripped over his wife when he was getting out of bed (traditional Japanese sleep on the floor). Robert fell into crisis, thinking: *masters don't trip over their wives!* He had to confront whether or not to give up his teacher or change his definition of master. He concluded that Ueshiba's teaching was far too valuable to give up, and so he decided that masters sometimes trip over their wives and can still be unparalleled in their field. This story helps us ground our idea of mastery into a more human form and yet still demand of masters a level of skill and experiential understanding that is not only uncommon but that requires a masterful ability to do things others just cannot. Otherwise, why call it mastery?

We could hold mastery as just having a little skill in one small area of a field or perhaps as just the title for someone with a certain level of education or seniority or status. These are also disempowering views because they downgrade the idea of mastery to mediocrity or lessen the demands to simply time put in. Mastery should be the zenith of an uncommon level of skill. It should demand that the master transcend the limitations, barriers, and errors that plague others in that same endeavor. The standard shouldn't be lowered to create accessibility or ease of attainment. We also shouldn't hold mastery as unattainable or as pie in the sky. Having grounded this pursuit a bit, we need to get to work.

WHY SHOULD YOU PURSUE MASTERY?

One of the most common dispositions people have in regard to mastery is that it just isn't possible for them. From this perspective, you are unlikely to attempt such an undertaking. There are many reasons to pursue mastery, but the first thing that has to occur is you must view mastery as possible and possible for you personally. The idea that only special people, or particularly talented people, or geniuses, or people somehow born to be a master, can obtain mastery—all that must be expunged. My position on the matter is that if you have a body that works, a mind that functions, and the ability to learn, you can master something. Anything another human can do, you can do, because you are human.

Why should you pursue mastery? Simply pursuing mastery changes and improves your life, even before any attainment. It forces you to question and thoroughly investigate your field, your own mind and/ or body, and your relationship to whatever you encounter—in your field and beyond. Just shifting your experience to that of one who is pursuing mastery puts you into a positive and capable frame of mind. That alone produces a positive change of state and gives purpose to your life.

As you question, investigate, and practice you will discover overlooked aspects of your own mind or body. You will discover assumptions you have that produce ineffective results; once discovered, you can stop assuming them. Your sense of wonder and curiosity increases considerably, including about areas you didn't even notice prior to undertaking this pursuit. From this wonder and investigation, you'll develop a deeper understanding and creativity, not just of your endeavor but of yourself and life in the process. From the progress you make pursuing mastery, you will create a deeper satisfaction in your living and much higher self-esteem. Plus, you'll develop greater skill as you go.

Attaining mastery moves you into a new world of experience. You must personally align with the principles necessary for mastery, and this creates a powerful new experience. You learn to surrender to the demands of these principles—thus creating commensurate states of mind—and this provides clarity about what to do and how to be. You aren't subject to mere reactivity or guessing or a hit-or-miss approach. Perhaps the greatest aspect of mastery is the freeing and transcendent experience you have when you surrender to it.

The overall purpose for most people—although it appears in very different forms and with various objectives—is probably an enhancement of their experience of life. You'll find that greater health, strength, and vitality, increased awareness and capacity, and better relational sensitivity and responsiveness—all appear as possible in this pursuit. Yet there may be even more to it than what you think.

In order to communicate all that's involved within this pursuit, I need to address subjects that could sound abstract and be difficult to grasp without contemplation, study, and insight. This may start with the very next segment. But even if this or any segment isn't fully comprehended, it still serves as a useful consideration to help open up and exercise your mind to better hear all that is to come throughout the book.

> *Beethoven said that it's better to hit the wrong note confidently, than hit the right note unconfidently.*
> MIKE NORTON

Practice, Principle, Being

When it comes to creating mastery, there are three stages that need to become a natural part of your experience. Everyone knows that in any art, sport, or endeavor, "practice"—repeatedly engaging in actions attempting to be effective in some way—is essential to the process of becoming skillful. The statement "practice makes perfect" embodies this sentiment. What most people overlook, however, is that it isn't just practice alone that gets the job done. When someone masters something they have consciously, or unconsciously, made two more shifts.

Practice implies lots of repetition, doing something again and again attempting to accomplish a result—often falling short, making corrections, and trying again. Over time you begin to improve, but an even more significant shift starts to emerge. After some success within various circumstances, you may begin to become privy to the principle(s) behind how this activity works.

Consciously searching for and contemplating the principles that determine success greatly increases your likelihood of finding them. Once you experience a principle you can then begin to act from that principle. When an effective principle governs your actions, success is almost inevitable.

Before going into specific principles, perhaps it would be useful to consider what I'm referring to *as* a principle. Let's start by looking again at traditional definitions of principle that may apply:

- a fundamental truth that serves as the foundation for a system of behavior or for a chain of reasoning
- a rule governing one's personal behavior
- a general scientific theorem or law that has numerous special applications across a wide field
- a natural law forming the basis for the construction or working of a machine
- a fundamental source or basis of something
- a fundamental quality or attribute determining the nature of something; an essence

ORIGIN from Latin *principium:* "source"; *principia* (plural): "foundations"

From the definitions, you should begin to glean what may constitute a principle. Here, a "principle" is what dominates your experience and actions so that these unfold in a particular way. The principle demands that your actions are consistent with it in order for it to manifest. Because the principle needs to dominate your actions in order for you to be effective, it must also dominate your experience. In order to do that, you have to experience what the principle really is as itself and adopt it.

In this way, your state of mind becomes consistent with the principle because your perceptions must recognize the distinctions that allow you to follow that principle. You'll perceive what's occurring in relation to the principle and take actions in response that are consistent with it; that is the function of adopting a principle. A principle demands an interaction must turn out a particular way without fail if it is to be consistent with the principle. To illustrate, I will use two examples of principles: gravity and honor. One is a law of physics, the other a social possibility.

You can see that as long as you're on this planet, you have no choice but to relate to the principle of gravity if you want to manage such acts as standing, walking, and so on. In our world, this principle is a given, and everyone must align to it in some way. To master an activity where gravity is a core element, however, you must refine and improve your relationship to it, and your every action needs to be dominated by that principle.

In the case of honor, this is a principle you have to adopt or create (rather than simply align to it as you must with gravity), and the only way it works is if you surrender to the demands of honor. You have honor only when it shows up in your experience and behavior and dictates what you do and don't do. The principle doesn't exist anywhere else, only in what you do, and yet the principle isn't the act itself; it is what dictates the act.

Adopting a principle means your experience can no longer be subject to the usual, seemingly random and self-oriented whims and impulses that are familiar and considered simply the private world of your inner self. This common self-experience is often thought to be the only possibility available for people—save for applying discipline and willpower to temporarily override it.

Yet consider a new possibility, such as adopting a principle that is as solid as gravity to dominate your entire experience. You can see that with gravity things always fall down, and everything is aligned with this force. Avoiding gravity is not an option. As long as the principle is active, all experience and action will be aligned with it and dominated by it. It has to be the same for any adopted principles if they are going to be effective.

You can't be effective with any principle unless you experience it for what it is. This means separating out any baggage the word or concept might bring along. If you only intellectually or conceptually understand the principle, you will fail to make it work. For pursing mastery, a principle cannot be about morality or beliefs. It can't be grasped if you add personal reactions.

A principle doesn't care about you, nor is it necessarily designed to benefit you or your agenda. The principle may well not be consistent with your belief systems, and you should not try to fit it into your views about the way the world should work. When everything that is not simply and only the principle itself is stripped away, you are left with the principle. A principle is a principle. It is not good or bad; it is simply *that*.

Of course, you adopt a principle to serve you, but it won't serve you and has no real power if it isn't allowed to be what it is. It won't work if you don't experience and surrender to it *as* itself. This means you must let go of anything inconsistent with the principle, even if you desire for it to be otherwise.

It is important that you *experience* the principle, not just understand it, and that your disposition, state, and actions are dominated by and consistent with it. When you do that, your experience will be different, you will recognize the principle acting in relation to circumstance, and you will immediately have different results.

Let's look more deeply into the two aforementioned examples of principles to see how they would show up in your experience. Starting with the principle of gravity, you can see that every physical action you take on this planet revolves around aligning with gravity. Since you were born this has been the case, and although you may not remember, you practiced again and again to align with and master this principle. Eventually you became successful at performing the actions you were attempting—standing, walking, and so on. But because all of this was done without any real consciousness of the principle, except for the demands it placed on you, you may have stopped progressing to a more refined degree once you mastered the basics.

If you were to take up tightrope walking, for example, you would find that more practice and probably more conscious sensitivity would be necessary to have success in that art and certainly to attain mastery in it. When you consciously search out an experience of the principle, you can improve, and even master, your relationship to gravity so that your physical actions are perfectly aligned with the principle, and you can perform feats related to gravity that most people can't.

Yet there are many principles that don't require alignment to physics. These include socially created principles or principles that apply to both physical and nonphysical arenas. There are also probably principles operating in your field that you don't even know about. Mastery demands that this condition of ignorance change. Whatever principles are required to effectively produce results in the endeavor you're trying to master need to be discovered, experienced, and adopted.

There are many principles that create powerful abilities in various domains—physical, social, business, mental, emotional, and so on. Many of the principles that work in the physical domain also work, in a different form, in mental, social, or business domains. A sampling of a few principles that make a significant difference in many domains are: listening, honesty, integrity, letting go, being calm, inclusion, acceptance, joining, and so on—and many other extremely effective principles we will look at later on.

To better ground how elective principles work, let's take a deeper look into the socially created principle I brought up earlier to see how it might affect your experience if adopted. Honor is a principle that may seem antiquated and receding as an active or common principle in our modern culture. When we hear a word such as honor, we immediately have ideas about what it means that are likely to include associations with morality and traditions. Yet if we are to experience the principle itself, we need to strip away all such associations or any other baggage that may be attached.

A principle doesn't have to "look" a certain way. When some so-called principle has to take a particular form then that would be a "tradition" or cultural custom or personal routine. These are not principles but dogmas or rituals. The principle, on the other hand, may or may not be operating within these rituals. A principle is what governs activity to unfold in a way consistent with the demands of that principle.

What is the principle of honor? For someone to have honor, it seems they must adhere to parameters of behavior that are confined to and demanded by the principle. Being honorable means being consistent with honest representation and principled interactions—doing the right thing, keeping your word, and conducting yourself in an honest and transparent manner. This means that something bigger than the impulses, desires, and needs of the self is the defining factor. Lying is unacceptable, deceit is beneath you, and doing anything to hurt someone behind their back is disgraceful. These things are just not done, even if doing so would benefit you and not doing so may bring you harm or discomfort. This principle creates a much larger sense of self because it is not restricted to individual needs and agendas but a far more inclusive, open, and transparent sense of being. Are you beginning to grasp the principle?

You need to take care not to conflate traditional affectations or stances with being honorable. They may or may not be. What makes them honorable is the principle governing your behavior, not the posturing or showy expressions. Honesty, doing the right thing (which is inclusive, serving everyone involved, not just an individual), fair play, being bound to one's word no matter what, being transparent and straightforward—these are all behaviors consistent with the principle of honor. Can you see the dramatic influence on your experience fully adopting this principle would have?

You might think that this principle would only affect your behavior, but this is far from true. Living and acting within the principle of honor requires that your thinking and emotions are also consistent with it. For example, an attitude of deceit would be seen as repugnant to you and so would be internally rejected. The thought to consider dishonorable behavior would be toxic and therefore either wouldn't arise, or if it did, would elicit feelings of guilt or shame and also be rejected. You can see that your thoughts and feelings would definitely be influenced by the principle.

What's more, self-esteem would rise dramatically, integrity would be an active aspect of your self-experience, and your internal state would tend to be consistent with your expressions, because you would be engaging far less in exclusive self-serving or deceitful expressions or impulses. So, the principle would definitely affect your internal state and self-experience as well as your behavior.

That is an example of one principle you can see would greatly influence your social experience and make a huge change to your self-experience and life experience. That's how principles work. Imagine what would occur if you adopted any of a number of principles, such as those mentioned earlier, and others specific to and effective in your domain of interaction.

In the fighting arts, for example, there are many principles that tremendously increase effectiveness. Just a few of these principles are relaxing, centering, being unified and whole, grounding, listening, yielding, joining, leading, and many others. Through the names alone you may be able to imagine some principle behind the words and perhaps imagine how they might contribute to your experience if you used them within a fighting context. You may also be able to consider how in a different way such principles might apply to your own field of interaction.

In any case, now that you have an idea of what a principle is and how an effective principle can change your experience, and thus your abilities, let's go back to the three stages that are needed for mastery. Again, the first stage is practice. With enough practice, and perhaps leaps of experiential insight, you begin to detect a principle or principles at work that determine the effectiveness of whatever you're practicing. Once you experience and can take a principle into action and validate its effectiveness, you are closing in on shifting to the next stage.

After you have practiced enough to discover the principle, and further, practiced enough to experience and prove the principle to yourself, you move into the stage of surrendering to it. Surrendering to the principle means you make the principle dominant over your internal state and actions. Once this is the case, you don't have to proceed in bits and pieces, deciding this or that, and taking shots in the dark in your interactions. The overall operational decisions are pretty much made since the principle decides and you simply choose the method of action. Once you surrender to the principle, you are now effective in any activity that relates to that principle. This is something you can do consciously and deliberately whenever appropriate.

Beyond this level of mastery, if you see a principle as a fundamental aspect you want to be central to your own self-experience and life, you can then adopt it as an aspect of yourself. In this way, you begin "living" the principle rather than simply adopting it to serve some particular domain or field. For example, perhaps you see that the principle of honesty is essential for an authentic experience of being alive and therefore decide to adopt and live within this principle as an aspect of your very person. At this point, there is no need to try to be honest, and no thought has to be given to it; it is just a clear and obvious aspect of your experience. This is "living as" or "being" the principle.

When it comes to mastering your domain of interaction—be it a physical activity, a social activity, a business activity, or what have you—absorbing the effective principles as a natural experience puts you into the place of mastery in that domain. To get there, your job is to practice, investigate, and discover the principles pertinent to your field. In all physical activities, or in just having a body, the principles found in my book *Zen Body-Being* apply no matter the activity. There are some principles that should relate to all endeavors, however, and as you read on you'll be introduced to many. Experiencing what they really are and bringing them into your field is up to you.

KNOWLEDGE USEFUL FOR MASTERY

Foundation Principles

The central principles and dynamics that I've seen are necessary to pursue mastery are a bit involved and seemingly enigmatic. As such, they require considerable contemplation and training—you have to throw yourself into experiencing what's what in order to understand it. If you are not ready to tackle such an undertaking at this time, I suggest you stay with the first section—"Mastery: The Short Version"—and come back to the rest of the book when you're ready to take it on.

Questioning

If you're ready to pursue such an investigation, you can start by contemplating questions such as: What is skill? Why is one person skillful and another not? What are the fundamental components necessary for creating a more effective learning that can lead to mastery? What is mastery? Investigate and contemplate these questions in relation to your field. Starting with the idea that mastery suggests being able to produce the results that you seek, consider how can this be done. Look into it, and begin the work.

The range of subjects this pursuit applies to is broad, but what's required of you may be greater or lesser depending on the demands of your endeavor. Effective interaction might apply to simply getting another to contribute to some process you have in mind, or to accomplishing consistently successful business outcomes, or to mastering an art—from a static endeavor such as painting, to a dynamic endeavor such as dance, or to a multidimensional endeavor such as real full-contact fighting. The demands for each are more or less complex or involved, but the desired outcome is to nonrandomly and consistently manage circumstances to produce results that are consistent with your purpose for the undertaking.

Purpose

Ask yourself: What is your *purpose* for pursuing your field? Once you are clear what your purpose is, whole sets of activities and views can get stripped away if you see they are not aligned with your purpose. Focus on whatever activities are left, making sure they are aligned with your purpose and to whatever objectives you assess will get you to mastery in your field. These objectives may be a best guess in the beginning, but as you progress, you can change them to be more accurate or realistic. If you find any activities that are not consistent with your purpose and objectives, toss them out.

Responsibility

Furthermore, in a quest such as mastery you must adopt an intimate and personal sense of *responsibility* for the investigation. You must be at the source of discovery and experience for yourself what is true and what is not. In my many decades of teaching, one thing has become clear: if the student does not take on the study, the pursuit, the task of learning and growing, as his or her own, then nothing can further their progress no matter what is said or done. Therefore, responsibility in the matter appears to be one of the fundamental requirements or components for developing ability. This cannot be overemphasized.

Remember to grasp the principle of responsibility. As with any principle, you need to do so without the baggage of attachments, such as cultural attitudes and assumptions, morality, burden or blame, and so on. Experience the real principle for itself. It is simply putting yourself in the driver's seat, so to speak. This means your disposition is one of pursuing mastery yourself, with the help of others if you can get it, but being undeterred even if you have to do it all by yourself. Whatever results you produce or fail to produce are yours without excuse or justification. You are the one pursuing mastery, and you own it.

Actions Relate to Perceptions

Another foundation principle to discover is one that usually goes unnoticed. It is that *your actions are determined by your perceptive-experience*. Unlike responsibility, this is one of those principles you don't have any choice about. Whatever you experience and how you experience it will determine the actions you take. In other words, whatever action your mind thinks is called for in relation to what you perceive, that is what you will do, and you have no choice about that. The intention to act relates to the perceived circumstance. How you assess what you experience determines what will arise as a feeling-impulse in your body that motivates the actions you take.

Without perception, what action would you take? You would take none. Without awareness, thinking, feeling, or experience, how would you direct action, movement, or process? You couldn't. For example, if you see a brick flying at your head, you will take action to get out of its path. If you see a ball coming your way, you may adjust your body to prepare to catch it. In either case, if you didn't perceive either brick or ball, you would take no action at all related to them. This principle is already at work and governs all of your actions. Think about it.

Feedback and Correction

As you take action in relation to someone or some event in order to accomplish a particular result, you also look for feedback about the action's effectiveness. Is it working? Depending on the activity, and the degree of your personal consciousness throughout the process, you'll search for success at various stages of the process as you go.

For example, in a golf swing, someone new to golf probably just swings and hopes for the best, then observes what happens as a result. On the other hand, a master golfer may well notice something is off even as she prepares to swing and so makes a correction; throughout the swing, she will sense error or success as it proceeds and may or may not be able to correct. In a business project, there may be weeks or months of process obtaining desired results leading to an ultimate objective. Throughout this process there will be feedback suggesting whether or not you are on track. The more successful businesspeople pay attention throughout the process, even to small shifts or subtle aspects that provide more nuanced feedback, so that they can alter their actions when needed.

You only change your actions if, in your experience, the feedback you get is that your actions aren't working out. There are many places you can look for improvement if and when your actions aren't producing the results that you want. You can try harder with the same actions, or you can try different actions. Perhaps you might attempt a new strategy or alter your current plans. Such correction might work, but these impulses and actions are all simply reactions to what has already presented itself to you as your options given what you experience to be the circumstance.

Altering your actions depends on your interpretation of the feedback. If this interpretation only modifies your experience slightly, then your actions will also only be a slight modification of what you were doing before. If that proves ineffective, you'll seem to be at a loss about how to proceed. You may work harder doing the same thing with the hope that repetition alone will make it work out. This approach is generally slow and painstaking, since you are trapped within the very framework and limitations that designed the ineffective relationship in the first place.

You overlook the fact that your actions are determined by and are commensurate with your experience. So it doesn't occur to you that if you change your experience you would change your actions. The possibility of changing your experience is not one that makes a lot of sense, because you undoubtedly hold that your perceptive-experience is a reflection of what is actually occurring. Yet if you look into this, you'll find it's simply not the case.

If you change or make any shift in your perceptions and experience, your actions will be different. If you perceive something you didn't before, you will now take action in relationship to that. If you stop adding some unnecessary element to your experience, then your actions will be freed from relating to that element.

Yet different is not necessarily effective or skillful. What you need is a shift in your experience so that your actions are now appropriate to accomplishing the task they are charged with accomplishing. You need to shift your actions from merely being related to what is *experienced* to being appropriately related to what is *occurring*.

So we see right off that the following are foundational to mastery:

1. Clarify your purpose, align to it, and toss all inappropriate actions.
2. Be responsible for your own progress.
3. Know that your actions already always relate to what you perceive and experience.
4. Understand that to be effective your actions must appropriately relate to what is actually occurring, therefore your experience must reflect what is occurring.

Knowing your purpose and clarifying your objectives allows you to know what's appropriate and what's not and tailor your actions accordingly. Responsibility puts you in the position where you are at the source of your thinking, actions, learning, and correcting, without which you can't master a thing. The fact that your actions are always related to your perceptive-experience means that how you experience things will determine your effectiveness. Finally, your experience and what is occurring aren't necessarily the same thing, and in order to be effective, you must relate to what's actually occurring.

This leaves you with the question: How can you transform your experience so that it immediately relates to what is actually occurring, such that your actions are always appropriate? That is a good question. It should be asked, not superficially, but contemplated and considered deeply until you have some experiential insights about the key parts of the question.

Yet in order for you to tackle such a transformation, it is useful to have some foundational understanding of how you create your experience in the first place. Some of the next few sections might seem a bit abstract, but if you ground them in relationship to your own experience, they can make a difference in your ability to make some changes.

How We Assess Ability

The principle of responsibility suggests that without moving ourselves into being at the source of our learning, mastery cannot occur. Yet we've all tried to change something in ourselves and fallen short or, after success for a time, reverted back to old ways. Changing our self-experience to one of being at the source of learning is not always easy or accessible, mostly because we are usually unaware of what it takes to do that. If we want to increase ability, it's useful to understand how ability is assessed in the first place.

Generally, what you consider to be your capacity is something you're already thinking, derived from a given set of beliefs and resulting in a perspective that occurs without reflection. This is a natural result of cultural thinking along with beliefs and assumptions you've developed as an individual from your personal history. Your assessment of your level of skill depends on how you currently experience yourself in comparison with everything else.

Skill is a function of a self and whatever that self is relating to—an object, an event, another. The other-than-self is experienced by the self, and so any action taken by you is taken in relation to your experience of the not-you. This whole experience is an interpretation. The interpretation is founded on comparing whatever perception and concepts you have of yourself to whatever you're relating to. This provides you with what you think are the possibilities for you to accomplish anything in relation to that subject, thus determining your sense of capacity in the matter.

For instance, say I decide to climb a tree. As I look around, I see a tree that is too small for me to climb. I immediately and without thinking regard the tree as worthless since it doesn't fit my immediate needs or the motivation for my search. I see the tree as unimportant, but my mood is only a mild dissatisfaction since I know that in the next instant I will move on to find a bigger tree, and that will occupy my attention. When I see a tree I can climb my mood shifts to excitement. I interpret the tree as a good one.

How do I determine that it is a climbing tree and that I'm capable of climbing it? As a constant, I live with the perception of my body. I am this tall and can reach so high, I can wrap my fingers and arms around things, my legs bend, I weigh such and such, and so on. These attributes are compared to the tree—it has large branches close to the ground, it is thick enough to support my weight, and so forth. Through this comparison, I assess that I can climb this tree.

Of course, I will also have intangible self-characteristics that contribute to my assessment of ability. For example, perhaps I am afraid of heights (a strange quality to have and climb trees, but perhaps I am also counterphobic). If so, I modify my sense of capacity to only climbing so far up. I also assess that I am smart enough to figure out a climbing pathway as I judge the distance between branches and create a strategy of how I can work my way up. All other relevant self-beliefs and assumptions, as well as beliefs and information (accurate or not) about how the physical world works, contribute to my assessment of capacity. Altogether, this process determines what will be experienced as my ability in the matter.

If you expand this example to include every element that makes up your interpretation of everything you relate to, you can see it is immense and complex. You also see something of the nature and dynamic of how your experience is constructed and how it relates to capacity and skill. The beneficial aspect of using examples is that they ground the consideration in something more easily grasped so they can be seen as real to you. Yet the danger is that people tend to limit themselves to and orient themselves through the specific example used. In this case, the danger of this is quite minimized, though, because your field of interaction will likely not be about climbing trees, and you must translate the example to relate to your field. I recommend that you use examples only as a springboard to create an experience of what is being communicated, and then apply this to your field.

Again, your abilities are determined by relating your self-experience to your assessment of circumstance. Whenever any situation, person, or event comes into view, your interpretation of what is there is immediately and reflexively compared to your self-experience. This happens so automatically and unconsciously that the experience of what's there is infused with this comparison, and the assessments, meanings, and mental-emotional reactions that result from this comparison habitually arise in your experience as you relate to what's perceived. Because of the automatic and unconscious nature of this process, you will simply assume that what's experienced is "caused" by what's perceived.

The convictions and assessments you have regarding yourself will determine whether or not you will pursue or not pursue any activity. Can you see that? What would you not even consider doing? For example, if you think of yourself as a shy person, you are not likely to consider that you are capable of any activity that involves performing in front of lots of people or forcefully confronting others. On the other hand, what do you think you could do?

Your convictions about yourself also determine *how* it is you will pursue something. They establish what you think is possible for you in relation to anything encountered and also establish how you will go about relating to it. This then determines the parameters of your sense of ability. If this self-experience remains fixed, then so does your ability.

Unfortunately, within this automatic self-referencing activity, what's encountered is not experienced for itself or as what's occurring. As noted earlier, to be effective you need your experience to relate to what is actually occurring. The instant you come in contact with anything you have already *not* experienced it for itself, but instead as it relates to your experience and beliefs regarding yourself, any action you take will be determined by this interpretation. Therefore, it appears that your fundamental assumptions regarding the way you are have a great deal to do with determining your abilities. Rather circular, isn't it?

Usually people think that ability comes from inherent talent. But if you don't have such a gift, this view cuts off access to mastery. On the other hand, if you're not limited to set patterns of thinking, or by a reactive relationship to circumstance, you have more room in your experience for the possibility of being competent.

Ability is seen as a comparative phenomenon, as "better than" or "worse than." People often think that ability is something that exists on its own—that you either have it or you don't. Actually, without comparative evaluation everything that you do could be called ability; simply doing something implies the ability to do it. Yet to consider obtaining an ability you don't have, you have to conceive of an outcome you aren't producing or can't produce presently. This means you must create a new possibility.

Although this next point may seem out there, perhaps a new perspective can add to our ability to create. When we delve more deeply into this point, we encounter a paradoxical truth about the nature of our reality that applies to our pursuit of mastery: possibility and limitation exist together. Anything that exists must be limited to the parameters of its existence. This very limitation is the possibility that allows for it to exist.

When some new possibility arises, it can't take its place in reality unless it takes some form. Once it's formed, that form is what manifests the possibility, but it also reduces the possibility to a particular structure—which is a limitation. To be actualized, a possibility is always wed to limitation—they are inseparable.

For example, perhaps we create the possibility of going to the moon. The possibility exists the moment someone has the idea that it is possible. But getting there is another matter. So, how can we get there? In any way that makes it happen. It is open-ended.

We could invent a rocket to fly someone there, or create a form of teleportation, or perhaps use astral projection, or maybe create a light beam that carries someone's molecules there, or perhaps grasp that we are already there somehow. We could invent an infinite number of methods, even ones we can't presently think of or that stretch the bounds of imagination or practicality. Whatever method we invent, however, the moment it is used we are limited to that method if we're going to make it happen. This invention may work to get someone to the moon, and so realize the possibility, but it is limited to that particular activity and process—as long as we use it. Otherwise it won't work.

It doesn't have to remain the sole method, however. We could invent other methods. But we often forget this fact because we get set in our ways, and it's easier to do what has already been done and established. This further limits our abilities and creativity and squelches open investigation. But no matter what we do, it always takes some form. That's how we actualize anything.

In the domain of skill or mastery it is the same. We have to adopt a particular strategy and take specific actions, but at the same time we could adopt many different strategies or actions. If we keep that in mind, even as we proceed with our actions, we are more capable of changing if appropriate or learning on the spot.

Your experience of yourself is usually quite limited to whatever form you experience as the way you are and beliefs you've adopted about yourself. This then creates your current experience of ability, and if you can't create the space to change what needs to be changed in order to pursue mastery, then you are rather stuck. Remember, self-imposed limitations aren't fixed, and you can realize the possibility of mastery by allowing your self-experience to change. Getting free of dysfunctional assumptions about yourself opens a door through which mastery can enter.

When your experience is dependent on relating everything to yourself, this forms the "perceptive-experience" from which you will interact or take action. If you create the possibility of changing your experience of yourself to some degree, you simultaneously alter your experience of everything else. Through this possibility mastery can be created.

The Possibility of Changing Your Experience

As we've seen, your actions are determined by your perceptive-experience, and to be effective your actions must be determined by what's occurring. Therefore, you need to change your experience to reflect what's objectively there and not what's subjectively added. You should do the same thing with your self-experience, since it's your self-experience that is compared to and related to anything encountered, forming your assessment of available options. Being burdened with a lot of subjective assumptions doesn't serve effective interaction, so one task is to get down to a more existential assessment of yourself.

To empower your movement toward that end, make the following distinctions in your experience:

1. A fundamental observation of being: *I am.*
2. An assessment and description of what is there: *I am small with little muscle.*
3. Judging what's described: *Being small and weak is bad.*
4. Managing what's judged: *Avoid anything requiring strength.*

In the distinction "I am," you experience existing as an entity, and this entity has a particular design to it—being human. Here, you have access to all possible abilities and capacities that exist within the human domain. Anything any human has ever done is possible for you, and you may also be able to do things no human has ever done. Therefore, your ability is rather open-ended and limited only by the constraints of being human, and maybe not even that—best not to presume to know where those limits are.

Who you are as a mere entity exists before any "knowing" or observation occurs. This place is open-ended as to what you can or can't do or how you must go about doing anything. It makes claim to very little in the way of particulars or limitations, and so to ability or lack of ability. An experience of being the one that you are is a particular experience yet one that is not closed or fixed. It is the most powerful and effective position from which to pursue mastery.

In the next layer of your self-experience, you add to your experience—of the open-ended possibilities of a being human for-itself—a "description" of what's there forming an identity and character. Although there may be some objective or factual assessments, a great deal of this description, or self-concept, is quite subjective and built on many assumptions about your nature. Any core assumptions or beliefs you have that you are flawed or less than perfect in any way—and pretty much everyone has some of these—will demand an agenda of resolution. This agenda will strongly influence your experience and your assessments, adding an overlooked subjective layer on top of the experience of simply being human. (This is a complicated matter to understand; if you want more detail read my trilogy: *The Book of Not Knowing, Pursuing Consciousness,* and *The Genius of Being.*)

This describing is like an "eye looking at itself," so to speak. The view of looking at the eye is a reflection and is radically different in nature and content than the view the eye has looking out, or the experience of simply "being" an eye. This description of your self is a fundamental interpretation—which is highly conceptual and strongly influenced by beliefs and assumptions—resulting from looking at relevant "self" aspects from a particular point of view rather than being you without any description at all.

For example, whether I say, "I am a strong person, I'm intelligent, blessed, and God is on my side," or "I'm weak, inept, and dumb, and life has never given me a break," I have only described something. Of course, this is not the whole story—such self-descriptions go deep and wide, as I'm sure you can see in your own case—and yet much of it may not even be true. Such a characterization is also likely to be judged as good or bad, since such descriptions can only arise through comparison.

The adjectives you use to describe something are always a comparison to some other possible quality, and the automatic tendency is to always judge what you assess. Within this description, you can see that the thing now observed—yourself in this case—is limited to the extent of the description. The opinion that you are smart doesn't include the observation that you are uneducated and seem to have no curiosity at all. Yet you live with your experience of yourself as described by you—consciously or unconsciously.

> *If you are not willing to be a fool, you can't become a master.*
>
> JORDAN B. PETERSON

Notice that the experience of observing something is not the experience of *being* it. Being a mentally and emotionally strong person is in a different domain than observing a strong person. The person we're talking about may have no notion whatsoever about his or her qualities that we might describe in this way. They are simply "being" some way we see as strong, but they just experience whatever they experience and do what they do, perhaps without reflection.

A description may or may not be accurate, and what is present can always truthfully be described in different or even contradictory terms. A person may consider himself a strong and fast swimmer, but if this is based on the fact that his grandmother told him so when he was a little boy, it may be true that in comparison to others he is a very bad and slow swimmer. This suggests that the person is not the description, even if the description comes from the person.

It is this "known" subjective description that forms the foundation for assessing your ability. Thinking that the opinions, beliefs, and conclusions you have about yourself are what is actually there is a mistake. The truth of these conclusions is always questionable, but beyond question is the fact that they are not an *experience* of you, they are a description of what you believe and assume is true of you.

Throughout your life, you've made certain conclusions about what was observed as your capacity. This came from an amalgam of what was said about you, what was programmed into you, conclusions drawn from attempts you made to do something, assessments of success or failure, and so on. This did create a way of determining certain abilities, but as you've seen, it also formed the limitations you experience. It is only one set of possibilities, much of which may not be true. The experience of being an open-ended human is difficult to describe.

I have fought and defeated many men who were far bigger and much stronger than myself. If I had in mind that I couldn't possibly defeat them, they would have already won. Comparing myself to them, I clearly came up short in size, weight, and strength. If my sense of ability were based solely on these elements, how would I even proceed? I would either quit right away or simply wait for my defeat to occur. Of course, this was not the case. I included those factors and adjusted for them—for example, not letting them use their strength or weight against me—and included every other relevant factor as well. Since everyone can be defeated, it was up to me to find a way to defeat them, which I did. The moral to this story is that limiting yourself to your habitual description is a bad idea.

As I mentioned, the third distinction jumps from describing the self to judging this description. This additional activity solidifies the description, and so allows no real access to shifting or changing the description itself. Judgment also makes the description right or wrong, good or bad, and determines what should be embraced, hidden, rejected, or managed about oneself. You can see in the examples above that inherent in your thinking is judgment. By judging I mean to evaluate everything in terms of right and wrong, and good and bad, to assess what is perceived in terms of its value or lack of value.

We are so entrenched in judgment that it is very difficult for us to even think without positive and negative opinion. In fact, we might say that, for the most part, people often don't *think,* they *judge.* This activity moves us further from any authentic experience we could have of ourselves as a human being with open-ended potential.

When I say "I am good" or "I am bad," in whatever form it might take, I will not perceive what is just so about myself. This severely hampers my ability to change anything, but more importantly, it sets my predetermined conclusions and assumptions in cement—it must, because I'm not questioning what's true for me but judging what's already assessed as there.

The fourth distinction is still another step away from open possibility because it is founded on managing the judged description. Since this position is two times removed from living as a description, and three times removed from being as an open possibility, the job of authentically changing anything is extremely impaired and appears to us as not really possible. This, of course, does much to solidify the conviction that we are some particular way that is immutable. This "managing" position acts as a superficial manipulator, a pretender, achieving mere facelifts, minor alterations, and patchwork solutions. It is merely a rearrangement and management of the limitations inherent in what's assumed to be true about ourselves and our abilities.

This is the usual place where you'll attempt to achieve any new skill or ability, but it is founded on what's already preconceived and on the limitations of what's already been formed. So, ability in this domain looks like it has already been decided, and you merely proceed to accomplish what you can, given the limits you've set. This domain is a far cry from mastery.

To pursue mastery, I recommend that you move back into the inherent possibilities of simply being human, and create the possibility of new ways of thinking and being. Naturally, the next question is: How is this done? It's done first by recognizing and eliminating assumptions and beliefs, convictions and conclusions. Instead, if you can experience being at the source of those activities, you move from describing and judging to *being* and *creating*.

Beyond such subjective self-reflection and transformation, we must also look into the objective nature of process. All experience and action occurs as a process. Everything that happens occurs as a process. To master something means to master process.

How We Relate to Process

Everything we do is a process. When something occurs—when any activity takes place—it means that something is going through changes. For a body to travel, one foot is placed before the other, and so on. This is a process. When you think thought after thought to draw a conclusion, this is also a process. An emotion arising occurs as a process in itself, but interpreting its meaning and being motivated by the emotion to take action are continuing processes designed to produce the particular result intended by the generation of the emotion in the first place.

All activity occurs as process. Process is one event followed by others moving in a direction to accomplish some end. Everything we experience and everything we do is a process. How we *relate* to process makes a big difference in our experience and in our ability to manage circumstance. Process is not only relative; in human activity, it also proceeds toward a conceived purpose.

Our concerns related to process are seen most often in our ability or inability to produce results. But since our automatic focus is on managing circumstance, our attention often locks onto results in a less than effective way. We do manage to produce results, but frequently at the cost of much stress and strain. Our relationship to process, however—and so our effectiveness—might be improvable.

One thing we miss about results is that they are always a part of a process. We tend to think of a result as the outcome of a process or caused by a process, but that isn't the most effective way to relate to it. It is not something different from process—it *is* process. If two hydrogen atoms combine with an oxygen atom, water is formed, and so we say water is the result of this process. Yet the atoms may break apart and combine with others, or the water molecule may well combine with other molecules to produce various other substances, and so we might see the combining of hydrogen and oxygen as simply part of a process leading to different results. Process is ongoing and endless. Within this ceaseless stream, results come and go. Each result is solely a segment of continuing process.

When it comes to our volitional actions, a result is simply the part of a process we engaged the process to achieve, but it is still only a portion of the process. When we change or eliminate what we focus on as the result, we find that process continues and is ongoing even once the segment we call the result has come and gone. We hear in advice such as "swing through the ball" the suggestion that focusing on the process rather than the goal produces a better result.

The result we want to achieve could be any number of segments in a given process. For example, if I'm a worker at a Pepsi factory, results for me might be to get all the bottles loaded on a machine. If I'm the manager, perhaps my desired result is produced by buying the ingredients and making sure they are distributed to their proper stations. As the Pepsi factory owner, my result in the process might be for the factory to get out the finished product. But if I'm a Pepsi drinker, all of that would only be parts of a process to produce the result of drinking a soda.

Beyond perspective, another example can be found in a martial interaction, showing process doesn't stop, regardless of any results attained. If I aim to throw someone down, I will engage in actions toward that end. But even if I'm successful, once the person is on the ground, nothing stops. He will get up and we will continue, or I will drop on him, try for another result, and continue to engage whatever seems needed next. Even when the match is done, I will still engage in processes and results—by walking off the mat, taking a shower, driving home, eating food, and on and on. Not until I die will I stop purposefully engaging in process.

When we engage in any process—which occurs with everything we do—the reason we engage in it is to produce a result. To scratch an itch involves the process of lifting a hand, reaching a specific place, properly wiggling the finger, and feeling the sensation of the itch subside. This is called scratching an itch, but process doesn't stop with that. The hand lowers and goes back to doing something else or just hangs there for a bit, but these latter parts of the process are usually ignored because they don't relate to the desired result. This ignorance likewise accompanies the way we relate to problems.

In human affairs, whenever we have a problem, it's because a process we're encountering is producing an unwanted result. If the process is an activity we are doing, then the problem is seen to arise when the process moves in a direction that isn't producing the intended result. For example, if I enter the process of getting married and I am denied a marriage license for some reason, or my car breaks down on the way to the wedding, or my fiancé gets cold feet, these are seen as problems. None of these "problems" would be problems, however, if I hadn't started toward or desired a particular result in the first place. Our problems are inevitably the result of some previous solution or attempted solution.

The very notion of having a problem is based upon things not working out the way we want. Either this wanting has produced some solution that is breaking down or is attempting to generate a solution but that effort is being thwarted. Perhaps getting married is seen as a solution to my loneliness, so I'm trying to solve a condition that's seen as a problem. If the hose attached to my toilet leaks, it is a problem, but the problem wouldn't exist if the solution of managing human waste, and removing it from the house to disappear from sight and mind, wasn't first undertaken. Think about it: What human problem doesn't arise from some past or desired solution?

If a mountain falls on you, this doesn't seem to fit into the model, because a mountain falling isn't a human invention. But how often do mountains fall on you? Certainly, after erosion due to mining, perhaps your town could get buried in a mudslide, or maybe there could be an avalanche while you're skiing. But these are clearly related to human solutions—producing energy and enjoying recreation. Of course, we could say that a natural catastrophe is only a problem because we are trying to solve the ongoing problem of survival. Although true, we don't need to go that far. Overwhelmingly our problems arise from human solutions to something else. Even the problems of climate change are a result of solving energy acquisition. Can't get a signal for your cellphone? What solution produced *that* problem?

Solutions to manage our objective world, although abundant, are only part of the topic at hand. Language, culture, society, beliefs, religions, fantasies, and so on are all solutions to personal and human conditions of some kind and are held as improvements to our condition. Etiquette and being polite, for example, clearly provide solutions to accomplish partnership and physical and emotional safety in our interactions. And we can see that, although these are significant contributions to our social experience, such "rules of engagement" are only a fraction of the world we've created. Remember, every solution is subject to breakdown, and every desired result can be thwarted.

If we took away all attempts at producing results, we'd have no problems. Returning to an animal existence, we can see that even though life might be immensely simpler and we'd likely have very few problems, we would still strive for solutions to fulfill the need for shelter, food, and mating. Whatever solutions we come up with will open the door for breakdowns to occur.

Life demands solutions and breakdowns are inevitable. Despite that, how we relate to process and breakdown makes a big difference not only in our ability to relate effectively—in other words, being able to redirect the activity toward producing desired results—but also the level of stress or degree of satisfaction we will experience.

For example, often when we encounter a problem, our attention contracts into the place the problem is encountered. This is usually not the best place to focus for achieving a resolution in the matter. No problem occurs in isolation. Just as a result is a segment of a process, so is a problem. It represents a breakdown or impasse to achieving the intended result. But this point of contention is also the result of the occurring process, and it manifests only when activities indicate the desired result is impeded. Knowing how results occur allows us a different relationship to process and to life.

When we step back and look at the whole process, we can better see how it came to such a place. When we relate to the whole, we will see where the process went off-track as well as where it is now, and we can change our activities to adjust the process so that we can get back on track toward the desired result. This can happen in a very small moment of time if understood correctly. Still, even when we're not restricting our attention to a problem, we too often focus solely on the result, which, as mentioned, is usually a mistake.

The process that exists prior to any result is essential for producing that result. The more fluid we are with our attention and our ability to correct or change the ongoing process as it unfolds—from before the beginning to after the end—the more success and precision we can have in producing results. The finer and more accurate the distinctions we make in the processes involved in any endeavor, skill, or art we might undertake, the greater our mastery will be. (I will address this aspect of process more in the section "Objective Distinctions," p. 81.)

These same observations and dynamics hold true for all processes we engage. All physical actions occur as process but so does thinking, emotion, and every other subjective activity. The way we relate to each other or to any circumstance is subject to these same principles. No problem, breakdown, or result occurs on its own. They are solely a function of the processes that create them. They are all the result of whatever is taking place or unfolding. They are simply parts of a process.

If the occurring processes are not producing the results we want—in other words, are unfolding in a direction inconsistent with our desired objectives—we will call this a problem. If they are fulfilling our desires or intent, we call these results. By better understanding the nature of process we can better relate to the whole activity and be more effective at making our actions appropriate to what's occurring, nudging it toward the results that we seek. Skill or ability always and only show up as process. How people determine ability, and in this case, mastery, is a complex process that requires our further attention.

Chapter Four
The Principle of Effective Interaction

ISOLATING THE PRINCIPLE OF EFFECTIVE INTERACTION

Again, what constitutes whether some interaction works out well or not? Since an interaction is determined through the actions of the parties and elements involved, you must grasp how your actions contribute to or detract from the desired outcome. You must assume responsibility for the influence you have on the unfolding processes.

In order to grasp mastery, it's best to understand the dynamics and principles involved in doing so. Then, design your experience accordingly, and tailor your actions so that you're aligned with these dynamics and principles. Although simply stated, this is quite an undertaking.

The most important thing to remember is that any principle, to be effective, must be correctly understood and experienced. Defining or explaining something does very little good in itself—unless it's used as a springboard from which to jump to an experience. By "experience," one could think that I only mean to activate the principle and then experience it in operation. This is very important to do, but what I'm also saying is to experience the principle itself, not just the effects of the principle.

This distinction is difficult for most people to grasp. Either they fail to have any access to the principle because there is no "example" or visible thing to grasp, or they become abstract and intellectual with it, getting it only as a theory or concept—neither of which are very effective if the goal is mastery.

For example, seeing things fall down only indicates the principle of gravity if you attribute the falling to the idea of an unseen force. You're getting closer to grasping the principle itself when instead of observing that things fall down—which everyone on the planet does—you grasp that they don't fall up, or float, or go sideways, and so on. Do you see how this moves you toward an experience of the principle itself—not just the effects of it?

Another example might be some principle of communication such as listening. If this principle of listening demands that we actually "hear" or experience what is so for the other person being listened to, then if that doesn't take place, the principle isn't operating, is it? *What* is "heard" is irrelevant, only *that* it is heard and that it is what's experienced by the other. Looking like you are paying attention, gazing at the other person with interested eyes, and nodding as if you agree— none of these mean you are actually listening, just that you are going through the motions as if you are. The two are different. Grasping that the principle itself demands you actually experience whatever another is experiencing—*that* is what you must make sure happens if you want to adopt this principle.

Beyond these examples, when I speak about a principle, listen for the principle itself, not just the description. Let's start with a fundamental statement of the general principle of effective interaction:

> *Your actions must relate appropriately to the occurring event*
> *so that the purpose for the interaction is realized.*

Your actions must relate to and be designed by the others and circumstances you are interacting with such that your current objective is realized. One of the central operative words here is "by." Your actions must relate to and be designed *by* the occurring event. Consider that. How is it possible to have action designed by an event, let alone appropriately designed by an event? Digging into this principle warrants a more thorough investigation.

The "other" or "event" in the statement above refers to what is truly or actually occurring. In other words, your actions must be relating to what is actually taking place in the moment. As you've seen, this means you must accurately perceive what's occurring. Your actions must also be designed by—and so your perceptive-experience must be in touch with—what is effective for realizing your objectives in each particular moment of engagement.

Although you need to establish in your experience an effective criterion for determining greater and lesser priorities of importance in what's occurring, what affects an interaction is *everything* that is occurring. Whatever is occurring must be experienced, even if it doesn't seem that important. For example, in a fighting interaction, although the eye blinking may do little damage as an attacking element, to ignore it leaves out the fact that in the instant of blinking the opponent cannot see, and since his actions are governed a great deal by what he sees, this will influence what he can and will do. Likewise, his entire system is online, and even apparently disassociated activities are related to the interaction, if for no other reason than that they influence his overall experience. In other fields of interaction, different criteria and appropriate distinctions will dominate experience, but the principle is the same: notice everything.

To further unpack this principle, you need to again notice the difference between the principle that currently governs your actions—that your actions are related to your experience—and the principle of effective interaction. Relating to your *experience* isn't necessarily relating to what's *occurring*. In order to relate to what's occurring your experience must reflect exactly what's happening as it is happening.

The next thing you need to notice is that "appropriate" is an important element of the principle. There is much to grasp about what makes something appropriate. Toward that end, the first thing you need to know is that "appropriate" depends on the purpose for the interaction. The purpose determines the objectives, and action is appropriate if it is effectively and efficiently accomplishing these objectives.

To Recap the Basics

First, you must distinguish what "is" from your "experience" of what is, and grasp that those two can be different. Your experience includes layers that are not what is but many biased or reactive mental and emotional additions that aren't what's occurring, except in your own mind. You need to know that a reaction to something is not the thing itself and is a distracting addition to what's there.

You also need to confront that there may be data of which you are ignorant or are suppressing or overlooking. If so, these will be absent in your conscious experience of what's occurring, or they may alter it in an ineffective way. In this case, you have to become aware of whatever relates to your endeavor but of which you are currently unaware. Furthermore, your experience of anything is mostly an interpretation, and the interpretation you make depends on the framework in which you make it and the purpose for making it. Therefore, you must find an appropriate framework for the task at hand in which to interpret the activities. More on this later.

Once you have somehow transformed your experience into being presently reflective of what's occurring, it must also include all of the necessary distinctions that will allow for effective interaction within the field in which you're working. In the case of psycho-physical interactions, this means making clear objective (meaning physical) and non-objective distinctions. It is your experience of these distinctions that allows any strategy or course of action to be effective and appropriate.

Experience shows itself as thinking, feeling, emotion, attitudes, moods, interpretations, reactions, sensation, body-impulses, perceptions of any kind, and anything else that occurs within your field of awareness. I suggested that mastery for an individual can only occur if that individual is responsible for taking on a personal transformation of his or her experience regarding the content of their field. I stated that your actions are determined by your experience, and so your level of effectiveness is also determined by your experience. I asserted that your experience is stuck in inappropriate interpretations and is not an accurate representation of what's occurring. As suggested, this brings up the need to change your experience.

To further your pursuit of mastery I recommend developing the following:

1. A fundamental understanding of perception and interpretation that allows you to shift your experience to reflect what's occurring by eliminating all that is not simply and only what's there. Become aware of anything that is occurring of which you are ignorant. (This can be assisted by reading my books: *The Book of Not Knowing* and *The Genius of Being*.)

2. Once your experience reflects what's occurring and you perceive everything you need to know about the subject, then your actions should relate to your objectives. Therefore, a clarity of both your overall purpose and immediate objective is necessary, and a sensitive, constant, and overall awareness should be developed that instantaneously relates what's occurring to your objective. This will help determine whether or not actions you take are on track to produce the desired result. This has to become automatic.

3. It is essential that on the way to mastery you study feedback from your attempts and acknowledge errors so that you can correct your actions, perspectives, attitudes, or whatever else needs correction or inclusion.

DISSECTING THE PRINCIPLE OF EFFECTIVE INTERACTION

Let's break down this principle to get a better look at it. If an interaction is going to be effective, your actions must produce the results that you want. Taking the principle as "Your actions must relate appropriately to the occurring event," the operative elements are "action," "relate," "appropriate," and "event."

Your Actions

"Action" is what you do, be it physical or mental-emotional activity. When it comes to action, one place most people fall short is not including the whole system that is involved in the action. Instead, they focus on just the aspect they think will get the job done. For example, with a physical action, using the whole body is usually very important, even if an arm seems to be the main player. But beyond the whole body, the entire system includes balance, alignment, structure, sensitivity, perception, state of mind, thought processes, attention, and so on.

Restricting an action to just the arm denies all of the other factors the arm depends on to be successful. Adjusting any or all of those co-occurring factors will make a difference in how well the arm performs, increasing the chances of success. Also, responding to feedback that suggests your actions aren't working out shouldn't be restricted to simply adjusting the ending action you took. Rather, you should inspect the whole process and make adjustments throughout the activity as is appropriate.

Increasing balance or changing your state of mind, for example, can have more of an effect than merely moving the arm a different way. (For more details on effective physical actions, once again, I refer you to *Zen Body-Being*.) As for domains that aren't primarily physical, such as business or teaching, where communication is often the main activity, the same principle applies. Simply altering what you say, for instance, trying to create a short-term result, is often too limited. If you include changing how you think, your state of mind, your passion, the frame of your presentation, or what have you, the communication is probably going to have a far greater impact.

We've all heard phrases like "mind over matter," or "the pen is mightier than the sword." Such notions suggest that what is done with the mind has the greatest influence on success. But in my experience, nobody really believes it—even when they believe it. It remains a good idea but not a reality. This isn't a useful disposition, because your state of mind and perspective have a huge influence on your actions. (This will be addressed in more detail later on.)

Actions you take include mental, emotional, verbal, and physical activities. No matter what field you're in, the awareness of your actions must always include the entire spectrum of these experiential activities. Yet if your actions and activities don't relate appropriately to what's happening, they can't be effective.

Must Relate

Since your actions need to relate to what's there, what is meant by "relate"? "Relate" means "make a connection between." Here, this means making a connection between your actions and whatever is there. Your actions must correspond with and relate to what's occurring in a way that produces particular results.

> ### Your actions must continuously and commensurately relate to what is occurring.

As I will introduce in more detail later, some principles that greatly assist this are to "listen to" and "follow" whatever is happening. "Listening," in this case, refers to being fully attentive to and experientially in touch with what is actually taking place. "Following" means to move in concert with the movement or activity of others or events. This keeps you powerfully involved and in touch with whatever is arising, or every action taken, so that you can relate effectively to it. In any domain, listening and following mean staying in touch with every aspect of whatever is arising as it arises and taking action or making adjustments in concert with every part of the unfolding process. Can you see how powerful that alone would be? How can you apply these principles to your field of mastery?

Appropriately

The purpose for the interaction determines what is "appropriate" and so will determine the course of the interaction. The purpose is why an engagement is taking place at all. It is why the parties or objects involved are gathering and interacting in the first place. What determines whether the interaction is proceeding effectively or not is if your objectives for the interaction are being realized. If your actions are in the process of realizing the goals and objectives that are aligned with your purpose, then the actions are assessed as appropriate.

For example, say I want to have a loving relationship with a woman. My first action might be to ask her out on a date. If that occurs, I will consider my action appropriate to my purpose—and myself lucky. As we date, I take actions to endear her to me and invite more and more intimacy and communication and point out where our goals and world perspectives align. If I find an action backfires and produces a result that pushes her away, I will see that action as ineffective and make a correction. As long as my actions proceed toward the purpose for engagement they will be seen as effective and appropriate.

For further clarity, let's make a distinction between a goal and a purpose. Goal and purpose are not the same thing. A goal is a specific result you want to attain. Purpose, on the other hand, is the reason you are engaging in an activity or pursuit or the reason for which something exists or has been created.

As an example, let's say you take up running. Your purpose might be to become stronger and healthier. And a goal could be to be able to run a marathon. Working toward the goal of running a marathon is consistent with your purpose. Yet once you achieve this goal the purpose doesn't end, but continues toward the next goal(s). See the difference? As long as you are becoming stronger and healthier you are on purpose. Your objectives are also on purpose if they support this happening, and if so, then they are appropriate.

Goals and objectives are a subset or tool of the purpose; they represent activities and aims that are either on purpose or not. If they are on purpose they are in the process of, and being consistent with, realizing the purpose for doing whatever you are doing. If they are not, then they are off purpose.

Of course, the trick is to know beforehand whether or not an action is going to be effective so you can choose appropriately. Just keeping in mind the question—"Is this activity on purpose—is it relating to realizing the objective?"—helps a great deal to increase your level of sensitivity to whether each action is appropriate or not. If the action is not in the process of realizing the objective, it is not appropriate.

For example, in a dialogue, if I want to get clear on something being communicated and I start talking about the weather, or I walk away from the communicator, or I try to turn the dialogue into scolding the speaker in some way, all of these activities are inappropriate. To be appropriate, I must speak and listen in a way that produces clarity in my experience about the communication. Any other activity is off purpose and therefore inappropriate, and it shouldn't be done at that time.

If your actions are going to be effective, they must relate appropriately to whatever is unfolding. In many endeavors, you have time and opportunity to reflect on and think about all of this. In some interactions, however, such as physical combat, you must be able to determine these things within a millisecond or faster. How can this be done? We'll look further into this capacity later in the book.

If any action is going to be assessed as effective, it will be because the results produced by the action turned out consistent with what you wanted to have occur. Either that or you lie about it. Given that you don't distort or fool yourself about what really happened (which is a big given), the impact your actions have on the event will consistently be effective only if your actions are related to what's actually occurring. This important element of being appropriate needs a lot more explanation. Many new distinctions and relationships need to be worked out. That job will be tackled more and more as you go through the rest of the book.

To the Occurring Event

If you are acting in relationship to something that is not actually the circumstance—such as a reaction or judgment, an abstract thought or image, an assumption or belief, an illusion or a mistaken perception, a projection or ignorance—then you will be acting in relation to something that is *not* the "event." Thus, you will be less effective. So, the first requirement is getting what is actually occurring, and only what is occurring. Sometimes this can be a challenging task, and yet it must happen in one stroke.

Your concern here is to experience what is actually taking place without alteration or adulteration, beyond bias, and free from reactions or filters, perceptions of good or bad, senses of values or threats, or plans or personal preferences. What is there when what "is" is left alone? What is the truth of the matter?

What normally occurs is an automatic, habitual, and massive application of interpretation and bias to anything perceived. You judge, extrapolate, resist, figure out, find value, avoid threat, and apply an endless stream of conceptual-emotional processes to what is merely perceived, and then you react and act in relation to this experience. These additions always get in the way of a clear experience of what's there. You need to ask: What would be experienced if nothing extra were applied? You also need to grasp that such an experience will be very different than your usual experience.

As a base, your experience should be without reaction or bias. Since normally you don't experience anything without personal bias or reaction, or without applying your beliefs, fears, and desires, such an experience would be quite unusual. It would be totally useless to your personal self-serving needs and historical agenda. So why would you want that? You wouldn't. However, you need to ascertain what is actually there as itself in order to pursue mastery. If you could get beyond projection or bias in your perception, you would be much closer to the mere experience or "reflection" of what's there.

Yet you will continue to interpret and plan, and try to fit what's there into your plans, making the task all the more difficult. To address this impasse, you need to both see what is actually there *and* relate it to your objectives. You should notice, however, that relating what's there to your objectives—even though these objectives may be beneficial to you—is *not* relating what's there to yourself or your personal agenda.

Your brain is already very good at relating everything automatically to yourself and your self-needs. The difference here is you aren't relating what's there to your *self* but to your *objectives*. You must make a distinction between self and objective, and channel your perceptive-experience to relate to your objective, absent all of the reactivity and bias that comes about through relating it to your "self."

Keeping your attention riveted in every changing moment on what is impartially there, without charge or meaning, is the first requirement. This enables you to relate such an experience to your objective. But even this change in perception demands a great deal of skill and so requires practice and training. This "leaving alone" looks like a fundamental requirement for aligning with the principle of effective interaction.

Having an experience of an object, person, idea, feeling, activity, or anything else, as it is in this moment, is your goal here. When you start looking into the principle involved, you may see another commensurate sub-principle arise that could be called "letting go." In order to align with the principle of letting something be "as is," you need to let go of activities that aren't simply an experience of what's occurring.

"Letting go" means allowing the subject in question to be unfettered, uncontrolled, and undirected. It is allowing the subject—person, thing, event, thought—to go wherever, do whatever, or be however *it* wants. Whatever hold, will, or control that may be applied by you consciously or unconsciously is released, without trying to influence what will occur when that happens.

For example, when you let go of the tension in your shoulders, the muscles will fall wherever they fall. Letting go of insisting a belief is true releases you from it and creates openness in the matter. Letting go allows the activity that's happening to be experienced in its natural state as it is.

From this experience and freedom, you can more accurately, clearly, and appropriately apply any action that will lead to your objective. Letting be and letting go may seem unusual principles to operate from, but as you proceed you will see the need for them arising in many cases, especially when they are needed in order to engage other principles that depend on such activities.

TAILORING YOUR ACTIONS TO YOUR OBJECTIVE

Once you've established the ability to experience what's actually occurring, you've seen the second requirement is to have your every action and thinking be related to and dictated by this experience. In the case of a fighting interaction, for example, your actions must be taken only in relation to and as determined by the opponent in every moment. In this way, your actions will be relating to and in alignment with what is occurring. By engaging a principle such as the aforementioned following, your actions will always be designed by what is occurring in each moment—it is inherent in following. But this understanding isn't widely shared, and people tend to involve themselves in self-generated activities rather than relating solely to what's occurring.

If the field you're attempting to master involves people, experience an ongoing recognition of what they are doing, thinking, and feeling, and tailor your actions to relate to them, and your actions will be designed by what is occurring. This could be misunderstood, however, so again, make sure not to hear this as relating all that to you—trying to be liked, getting your way, being a doormat, getting upset, or what have you—but to your objectives. If no people are involved in your field, then tailor your actions to the objects or activities that comprise it.

You saw that the next requirement of the principle of effective interaction brings appropriate action into your consideration. Knowing what is there, and even relating to or having your actions designed by what is there, still doesn't demand that you are *appropriately* relating to what is there.

Your actions must serve the objectives of the interaction to be appropriate. Having a clear experiential understanding of what your objective is in any moment is important for taking actions to realize that objective. In a competitive context, this means you must also maintain an advantage in the relating, since the objective will involve some form of winning.

Once, when I was training a group of martial artists who wanted to go to the next full-contact World Championships, one man from New York City made an observation he shared with the group. He pointed out that "Ralston doesn't do anything that isn't on purpose; he doesn't waste movements on anything other than purposeful action in each moment." He was pointing out that the others did not adhere to this principle, that too much of their activity wasn't precisely relating to their opponent, and so they were less effective. This is an example of maintaining appropriate action. Discerning what that is may be the tricky part, but engaging the principles discussed so far brings you to the threshold of appropriate relating.

Although being clear about your purpose and objectives is essential, you must also remain open as to the form in which these might be realized. When you get clear on an objective, you'll often imagine what it will look like to accomplish it. This objective will be pursued through a string of goals that you imagine will get you there. These goals are accompanied by a strategy or plan you formulate in order to reach them. This is not a bad thing—in fact, it is necessary—but a danger exists when you lose track of the fact that what's imagined may not be what's needed.

Your purpose, and even your specific goals, almost never demand a particular form take place. The form, procedure, and goals, and so the strategy and plan, are open and often infinite in possible variations. When you fixate on one strategy, or one image or form, you limit yourself to this and drastically restrict your possibilities. The strategy then becomes your objective and so your objective ends up serving the strategy, rather than the strategy serving the objective. This should never be done. Strategy, plans, and goals only exist to serve an objective; never make the strategy the objective. There are many possible plans that can realize the same ends, and so the strategy needs to be open to change.

How do you tailor your actions to effectively obtain your objective? Once you are clear as to what is occurring, instantly compare it to the objective. A string of thoughts will occur, conceiving some process that you think should realize the goal you're pursuing. This may go on swiftly and almost without notice. If your actions are not in the process of realizing that goal, or do not look like they will realize it following your present course, then drop them and adopt a new course of action.

When comparing the occurring process with your objective(s), ascertain whether or not the process you're engaging is on track. A finely tuned sensitivity should arise from the ongoing comparison of process to objective, and this perceptive-sense needs to be a constant. When you detect that your actions are not serving your ends, make correction. Since this sense must include any changes that arise in the interaction, your plans must also change when needed, and so the possibility of adjusting your actions should also be constant.

Some of the Central Assertions Addressed So Far:

- You're responsible for being effective; you must be at the source of learning and mastery.
- Understanding and aligning with the elements that form being human—body, perception, mind, action, interpretation, anatomy, the physics and structural engineering of bodily design, and so on—allows you to be more effective within this foundational condition.
- Action arises solely in relation to perceptive-experience, so your experience must change in order to change your actions. Dwell on this reality and try to grasp the nature and implications of that fact.
- Action appropriately related to what's occurring indicates a principle in which mastery can occur.
- Mastery presupposes the possibility of transforming your experience—first, into an accurate reflection of what's occurring, and then, undergoing the training and adoption of a series of sophisticated distinctions that allow for you to quickly determine in every moment appropriate action that will produce results aligned with your objectives.

All mastery is about doing that which the senses tell us cannot be done.

Thomas Lloyd Qualls

In order to make your efforts practical and grounded, you need to make refined distinctions within the objective and non-objective—the physical and subjective—aspects of your endeavor.

Chapter Five

Transforming Your Perceptive-Experience

MAKING DISTINCTIONS

To accomplish what you've been exposed to so far and create mastery, work must be done to transfigure your experience. You need to make clear distinctions that will provide the information necessary to successfully reach your objectives. These distinctions constitute the perceived knowledge necessary to effectively relate to what's there.

To be clear, a distinction *is* whatever you experience in any way. Anything that is experienced or perceived—an object, a thought, an image, a relationship, a dimension, a feeling, emotion, numbers, words, ideas, space, anything experienced in any way or on any level—constitutes a distinction. Since distinctions make up your entire perceived experience, including mind, emotion, and internal states, then mastery demands that whatever distinctions are needed for effective interaction be known. Because your actions relate to your experience, your experience must be capable of relating effectively to what's occurring. What makes this possible is making the right distinctions. (For more on the nature of distinction see my books: *The Book of Not Knowing,* chapter 24, section: The Distinction "Distinction"; and *The Genius of Being,* chapter 3, section: "What Is a Distinction?")

When it comes to distinctions you already make, your job is often to refine and become more sensitive and sophisticated within that experience. For example, you make the distinction of, ergo experience, the weight of objects. Yet you may need to put more attention on having a very accurate feeling of the exact weight of something you're interacting with, keeping a constant and precise feeling-sensitivity of it, as well as knowing this weight's influence on and contribution to other elements involved in the interaction as a whole.

You also make a distinction between a feeling and an action, but when you confuse an emotional reaction with a physical action you experience a non-effective mush of two elements when you should be relating to only one. Have you ever been in bumper-to-bumper traffic and gotten angry? Why? In some weird way people think it will somehow make a difference and perhaps move the traffic. But this is confusing an emotion for action that does make a difference. In this case, usually the only consequence is adding stress and pain to your experience. Often, when action can be taken, such a conflation pushes action down an ineffective road. Other distinctions you haven't made will have to be made—such as grasping certain principles yet to be discovered or perceiving something you don't now perceive.

Generally, in your experience, you make a basic distinction between what is objective and what is non-objective. You distinguish between what exists as an object in the physical domain and what exists non-objectively as something intangible—such as thoughts, feelings, mind, perception, and so on. You must refine the distinctions of both the objective and non-objective domains so that your actions will relate to them with greater precision as they occur. If these new and refined distinctions constitute what must be known in order to be effective, then your actions will be effective.

In any physically interactive domain, there are many objective distinctions that need to be made, refined, and automatically included within your experience. But you should be clear: every interaction or field of skill is related to objects. In domains such as business, teaching, or social interactions, without the use of certain objects even the more nonphysical aspects that may dominate one's focus can't occur.

For example, if people are involved, then bodies are involved. You can't speak to anyone without some object, be it a body with a mouth and ears, a phone, or what have you. Although the main focus of a business meeting may be ideas and plans that exist in the abstract, the people involved still express themselves via their body language and presentation, and this will influence assessments of their character, their level of certainty, and so on. Whatever occurs in the business to create value will occur as a process involving objects in some way. In any sport the body obviously is used, but also often another object, such as a club or ball, must be mastered. With painting, a great sensitivity to brush, paint, and easel must be achieved. And so on.

If one is trying to master something like controlling one's mind or internal state, or perhaps master the emotional domain in some way, then no objects may be involved. But this effort at mastery will still relate to and have an effect on the body and probably your demeanor and interactions with others as well. All the abstract or nonphysical aspects of any interaction occur as a process, and the principles and distinctions that apply to the physical domain can often be applied to the nonphysical domain, and the nonphysical domain is frequently related to through objective metaphor or simile. So even if your field is not particularly physical, it is good to pay some attention to the physical domain.

OBJECTIVE DISTINCTIONS

Every aspect of the body exists to serve a purpose and is completely relational. Think about it. The body serves the purpose for which it was designed: interacting with the environment. We tend to think we exist as an object or self, independent of our relationship to anything else. But from head to toe, every system, every organ, every body part is designed to serve some purpose, and as a whole to relate to circumstances, other creatures, and the environment. The body exists to perform a function, which includes the non-objective aspects of the body, such as thinking, emoting, and perceiving.

Alignment with the body's design maximizes ability. Alignment with the principles involved in the most effective use of the body allows for perfect functional capacity. As I've suggested, for a more in-depth study of how to get the most from your body, read *Zen Body-Being*. Now, let's look into what makes up your experience of objective distinctions.

In your perceptive-experience of any physical interaction, to be effective you need to make clear distinctions. The demand to make objective distinctions may be greater in some fields than in others. If it's greater, more distinctions will be needed to be successful. To master any physical activity, you need to become fully conscious of your own body and the principles and distinctions involved in using the body. Then, depending on the activity, whatever the body is interacting with—gravity, space, a ball, another person, etc.—demands more sophisticated distinctions be made relative to that object.

Let's touch on some of the objective distinctions you might need to become aware of and sensitive to in your field:

1. Objective Qualities
   Weight
   Shape
   Design
   Substance
2. Space
   Three-Dimensional Awareness
   Distance
   Spatial Geometry

3. Process
   Movement
   Direction
   Relational Response
4. Force
   Balance
   Power
5. Timing

Depending on your field, but certainly in any physically based endeavor, every one of these distinctions needs to become part of your feeling-experience. Each should be trained to be part of a constant perception of whatever is occurring, and then fine-tuned to be very accurate and extremely sensitive. At first, I recommend looking into and training each distinction separately until it becomes strongly grounded in your experience. Then work at putting them all together into one experience. Continue to improve on each by taking them apart and putting them together again, increasing the degree of sophistication in your feeling-awareness of them. This kind of work may seem pedestrian and unglamorous, but a strong foundation is essential and the benefits will be remarkable.

Objective Qualities

You need to be able to feel and relate to the present condition of any object or body that is involved in your endeavor and always have a sensitive and comprehensive experience of your own body. Some of the most important distinctions of which you should increase your awareness are the weight, shape, design, and condition of the substance of the object or body that is involved in the endeavor.

The "weight" of the object needs to be constantly "felt" in your awareness, allowing for a much more effective relating to what's happening. For example, in combat, always being in touch with and "feeling" the weight of your opponent tells you where he is, the status of his balance from moment to moment, and the possibility of applying his weight or force onto you at any given moment. This keeps you in touch with what is happening with him as a weighted mass. This is very important, since it is largely through the use of his weight and mass that he can influence your body or bring harm. Even if he does not use weight to create harm, still his weight must accompany any movement he makes, and so will tell you where he is and what he is up to.

Even though you understand the distinction of weight, you may well have overlooked the many connections and relationships of which weight is a part. For example, the shape, balance, momentum, and location of an object are integrally connected to and affected by its weight and its weight influences all of these as well. Going forward, keep trying to uncover every interrelationship each element has with others. This is vital for mastery. Regardless of field, maintaining a sensitive feeling-awareness of the weight of a body, a ball, a club, a weapon, or even of an issue or assertion is an important factor for relating to it effectively.

The "shape" of any object determines much about its structural strengths and weaknesses and determines a great deal regarding its possible function. This being so, your relationship to any given shape must take this into account—be it a golf club, tennis racket, football, parachute, wave, horse, body, contractual proposal, communication, or something else.

In fighting, the opponent's shape will frequently change and sometimes continuously change. Thus, his structural strengths and weaknesses will change, and you must adjust your relationship accordingly. You know that at a certain speed, height, and angle a round ball will bounce so far and even at what arc—as long as you also know the substance of the surface it hits and the substance of the ball. On the other hand, an American football or rugby ball will react quite differently given its shape. Bringing shape into an instantaneous feeling-awareness includes the feeling-recognition of the inherent strengths and weaknesses of every shape in relation to you and your objective at the moment.

"Design" relates to shape. The distinction here, however, is the potential that the design of the object or body—or contract, or what have you—currently provides. For example, you may bend your arm so that the shape is an L, but the design of your arm is such that the elbow only bends one way. Whatever you are interacting with, its design tells you exactly what can and can't happen with it and what is likely or inevitable to happen given the circumstance. A bicycle's design gives a variety of possibilities in terms of gears and other components that must be known and related to with precision in order to be most effective. So it is with every object. With two people, depending on the relative positions of the two bodies and given how a human body is designed, some directions for movement will be more difficult than others. Given any particular posture that is taken, applying force will be easy at one angle while awkward at another, and so on.

For example, since, as we've seen, the elbow only bends one way, this limits what is possible for the use of the hand. If my body is positioned such that you cannot apply pressure without bending your arm, and your arm will not bend in the required direction, then you cannot apply pressure without readjusting your whole body structure. This provides a period of time for me to act that another position may not. Given the relative position and design of the joints and body parts, I may be somewhere in relation to you such that you cannot apply pressure without breaking your fingers, or perhaps you can grab but not push, or maybe an attack by you beyond a certain range would put your balance in jeopardy. Taking every possibility of this kind into account gives a great deal of information about what is possible from moment to moment as the changing structures continue to redesign the relationship.

This is not a simple consideration. The possibilities are almost endless. The relative possibilities provided by the functional design of two or more objects in relationship only exist for the period of time that this structure does not change. That could be in a millisecond or much longer. Therefore, if the possibilities shift every split second, you must constantly readjust your actions. Clearly, the amount of information is staggering. The only way you can effectively and intelligently handle such a sophisticated amount of data and possibilities, and take appropriate action, is to have the entire mass of information received in one feeling-distinction. I will talk more about that later on.

The last of the major objective qualities is the "substance" of the object. Primarily, this refers to the condition of the object, what it's made of, and the nature of the material. Is it hard, soft, dense, or flimsy? You need to ascertain, with feeling-awareness, the substance of the ground, a body, a ball, sometimes a weapon, or whatever objects you are dealing with.

You know that the substance of a brick is different than that of a Styrofoam cup—as is the design, shape, and weight—and if someone tosses one or the other to you your actions and expectations will be molded around this knowledge. If you are relating to another body, sometimes it is rigid, sometimes pliable. Some bodies are dense and some fragile, some are tense and others loose, and everybody can change their degree of tension from moment to moment. Actions done standing in mud won't be the same as actions done standing on concrete and so on. Your actions need to vary depending on the condition with which you're currently dealing.

In the non-objective domain you might consider if a person has "substance," or if they are solid, immoveable, or flexible, whether their argument is sound, and so on. How sensitive you are to any given condition will help determine the degree of effectiveness with which you can accomplish your objectives. You must determine distance, timing, and often direction, range, and various other factors, depending on the condition of the substance, and adjust these instantly when any change in the condition occurs. Once again, this must be brought into a feeling-sense of what is an appropriate relationship, given the data.

∼

Keep a feeling-connection with the weight,
shape, design, and substance of any object.

∼

Space

Within the distinction of space you should keep a "three-dimensional awareness." This will include the infinite possibilities inherent in three dimensions—such as distance, movement, spatial geometry, objects, and time. You are well served to increase the sensitivity of your feeling-awareness of space and everything that entails.

When it comes to your body, you should develop a three-dimensional feeling-awareness of the whole body throughout every cubic inch of it as well as a feeling of the space all around the body in every direction. This increases the effectiveness and capacity of the body as an operating system and provides a greater sensitivity to all current objective relationships.

Having an all-inclusive spatial feeling-awareness provides an endless variety of possible relationships among objects within this space. These relational possibilities I refer to as "spatial geometry" to indicate the linear, planer, and cubic relations possible relative to bodies and objects. Once again, to use one of my fields of interactive expertise: at any moment, I can move my hand to your head or my shoulder to your chest, and so on, and these actions indicate lines of possible movement. Now consider every possible line between every possible body part.

In a punch, for example, the distance between the two bodies determines the kind of punch that will be used. If you are very close a long straight punch is awkward and ineffective but a hook works well, and if you are farther away the reverse is true, but if you are too far then no punch can be thrown. Referring back to design, you can also see that distance and shape determine whether or not you can use an elbow, or a knee, and so on. Can you hug or just wave at each other? As the distance changes, the possibilities change.

You can see that one of the most powerful distinctions within the distinction of space is that of "distance." An accurate feeling-awareness of the ever-changing distance between objects, bodies, or body parts is invaluable for being effective. Continuing with a fighting example, you need to know and feel the immediately occurring distance between your partner's hand and your nose, between your center and his center, between your feet and his feet, and his elbow and your head, and so on. From this awareness, you can know the possibilities available, and given the distances at hand, you'll know what actions are needed to produce particular results. As all of this becomes one feeling-sense, information is given to your body-mind directly, replete with the sense of danger, opportunity, or neutrality.

In your field, what distances need to be taken into account? You have to know and be finely tuned to the distance involved in swinging an object, or between a body part and an object, and so on. In non-objective domains, distance might refer to how far off a goal is, or the degree of connectivity to another person or a process. Try to work out every possible distance and spatial relation in your field.

But why do we need to know all of this, you ask? In my field, if I am to respond to your actions, and I can only make out one domain of spatial relationship, then I can only respond within that domain. Other possible areas for movement or structural relations would not occur for me, and it would be literally impossible for me to initiate movement in certain patterns, directions, or areas of space. If, on the other hand, I can make out an infinite number of relations, then I can perceive and respond within a wide-open field of possibilities. Your field may not be as spatially demanding, but space will still be a factor that needs attention.

In order to develop a more grounded sense of the infinite possibilities available in three dimensions, consider the following exercise.

Picture being inside a large room. Now fill the room with marbles. Notice that the room holds a *lot* of marbles! If you trace the connection between one marble and another next to it, and so on, you can see a line of marbles starting anywhere in the room and going anywhere in the room. Think about it. How many lines can you form? Trillions. Remember, they don't have to be straight. A spiral and a circle are linear too. How many spirals can you create? Remember, the spiral doesn't have to stay in the same plane; it can move in a pattern that looks like a spring or a whirlpool and can bend or form many other possible patterns. Try to think it through, and get a feeling for the possibilities. Don't just take my word for it. How many planes can be formed in how many directions? What about spheres, cubes, and other shapes? Imagine you are inside this room and can feel all of these possibilities all around you, but instead of marbles make it air molecules, because you *are* inside space surrounded by air.

By thinking these relations through until your brain begins to hurt, you can develop a much more sophisticated sense of the possibilities that exist within three dimensions. Many people don't have any real idea, much less a functional feeling-sense, of what's available in the domain of space. Of course, much of what you can imagine won't appear as immediately useful to you, but even as a felt possibility it will influence your actions in ways you would never have thought of previously.

~

Stay constantly immersed in three-dimensional awareness, and feel changes in distance and spatial relations.

~

Process

As we touched on in the section "How We Relate to Process" (p. 58), anything that proceeds through time, or goes from one stage to another, is a process. "Movement" always occurs as a process. All actions are processes. Process is a given in any physical or non-objective interaction or activity. As mentioned earlier, developing a powerful relationship with this distinction will provide much greater effectiveness in any activity. I want to point out a few more observations regarding process that most people neglect to make.

First, what we're usually talking about when we speak of process is an event or sequence of activities that unfold in such a manner as to accomplish a result. The progression of actions or circumstances over time (and the timeframe may be incredibly small or long) is called process. The smallest action is a process. A whole encounter or interaction is also a process. The blink of an eye, taking a step, thinking, and breathing are all processes, as are climbing a mountain, winning a tennis match, or becoming the CEO of a company.

As any process unfolds, certain distinctions can be made within every segment of the process. For example, all processes always follow a sequence of distinctions, starting before the process begins. There is the beginning of the process, or its birth, followed by the formation or growing period of the process, then the maturing or result period, and finally the end of the process or its completion. Then, there is time after the end of that process. Each of these stages in a process provides different possibilities and reveals various opportunities and obstacles, strengths and weaknesses. Knowing this, you can more effectively design your action in relation to the stage of the process that is occurring.

For example, an oak tree growing from a seed is a process. If you don't want an oak tree in your yard, it's best to prevent the seed from taking root; if you want an oak tree, you'll have to find and nurture a seed. What the process needs to thrive in the sprouting stage is very different from what it will need in the mature tree stage. Destroying the tree early on as it pops up is easy, but doing so will take a lot more work after it has grown into a mature tree.

In any process, when you recognize the potential possibilities at each stage, you can more easily change or influence the process at that stage, or better prepare for what's next. When the process is at a mature stage, it is much more difficult to alter—either from the inside if you're engaged in it or the outside if you're not the one engaged in it. Being sensitive to what's available at every segment of the process gives a much stronger sense of what can and can't be done. Appropriately aligning with a process in each moment and stage makes you more effective, powerful, and precise.

Again, I want to underscore that all results are only process. There is no independent event or thing that is a result. It is only the part of a process you want to achieve and why you entered into that particular process in the first place—that's why you call it the result. Yet it is only process. If you neglect the rest of the process in favor of trying to accomplish the result prematurely, then your efforts will be forced and disharmony will occur in the unfolding activity. People often unknowingly follow this latter course of action, even though it demands strain and effort and is ineffective overall.

I'd like to insert a paragraph from Chozan Shissai,* a Japanese swordmaster of the 1700s, speaking of a state of mind needed to master process:

> As it is with archery it must be so: The will is firm, the form is correct, the life force fills the entire body and is lively, the nature of the bow is not violated, the bow and archer form a unity. When the bow is drawn, and the archer is completely with this action as the spirit fills heaven and earth, then the spirit is calm, nothing moves the thoughts, and the arrow is released spontaneously. After the shot, the archer is the same as before. If the archer's spirit blends into a union with bow and arrow, then the bow is also filled with this spirit and is an equally marvelous creature. If the bow is forcibly bent then the nature of the bow is violated, bow and archer oppose and contradict one another and there is no mutual permeation of their spirits. Instead the strength of the bow is inhibited, and is robbed of its power, and when that happens the arrow will not fulfill its function.

---

*There are various English editions available of his work *Tengu-geijutsu-ron,* translated as *The Demon's Sermon on the Martial Arts.*

When you are instead in the "place" of the process as it is unfolding, not trying to rush ahead to the result, you can proceed effortlessly and will not break the integrity of your own actions nor that of the interaction. For example, if I want to move you from one place to another and try to "force" you to be in the other place, I am not allowing you to be where you are, so my energy and attention are not focused where you are but where I want you to be. This creates strain. If, on the other hand, I keep my energy and attention with you in every moment of the process of moving you, then there will be no separation and no strain. When you arrive at the new location, so will I, and not a moment before. I will go more deeply into this principle in the section "Mind-Body Alignment Principle" (p. 150).

Furthermore, without thinking about it, people frequently tend to think of a process as somehow a "thing." For example, a punch, a pitch, and a dance move are often thought of as some "thing" that occurs. We can see this when we say: it *is* a jab, or it *is* a fastball, or it *is* a pirouette—as if it is that "thing." But this is not the case. They are not things; they are all processes.

When you see actions as only processes, your experience of and relationship to them change immediately. For one thing, you don't have to identify the "thing" that is occurring before you can take action. Is it a punch or a grab? Are they going to shake hands or wave? Are they asking a question to manipulate you or do they really want to know the answer? Whatever is arising in this moment is what is arising, and you can take action in relation to that without knowing what is going to be next. Then you don't unconsciously take for granted that it will arise like a "thing" that just is or isn't, but instead perceive it as a process you need to attend. This allows a great deal more sensitivity to opportunities that can be engaged in the process as it's occurring.

Also, when you think of process and result as separate events and focus primarily on the result, you are likely to be caught doing something at the wrong time, thus derailing or hampering your efforts. If change is needed, this orientation demands that you stop what you're doing in order to do something else. It makes you slow and awkward. Instead, if you keep relating to what's occurring *as it occurs* rather than fixating solely on the result, you can merely transfigure whatever action you're doing into whatever action is appropriate to the unfolding circumstance. In this way, you don't have to waste time and energy resisting or stopping anything. You can simply go right into the next action that is appropriate.

Another distinction to be made in any process is that of its "direction." Direction indicates where and in what manner a process is going to unfold. In my field, this is frequently seen as the line or course of action in which the other will move or apply a force. When he attacks me, for instance, he moves from over there to over here in a particular way, following a particular process. This direction is critical information to be in touch with, since my actions must relate to it.

Relative to this flow of activity, you will take action in response. The "relational response" of your action to the unfolding process could be called a tactic or maneuver. Knowing the advantages and disadvantages that are inherent in various relationships is important. Relating to any movement or process is done with another movement or process, and the relationship between these processes forms a tactic. For example, if you move toward me and I move at a ninety-degree angle to the line of your movement, this produces certain results. Moving at an angle away from or into your movement produces different results. Your objective creates a strategy for action that will determine particular responses. All of this must be developed into a feeling that senses appropriate relationships between action and response.

～

*Know the meaning of each stage of the occurring
process, and relate appropriately.*

～

Force

The first aspect of the distinction of force is rather unique since it relates to the binding quality that exists in all things. The second element is what we normally view as force, which is force created or used by you to accomplish something, or force used by others against you or in partnership with you.

The first aspect encompasses the attraction objects have for one another and the binding force they have within themselves. Gravity indicates this objective force, as does the intrinsic strength of any given object—which is the inherent binding quality the object has for itself and draws it to be that object with that particular substance and density. This same binding force distinction could also be applied in a different way to an idea, a feeling, and so on.

Studying and improving your relationship to this first aspect of force influences many elements in any physical endeavor and in different ways influences nonphysical endeavors. For example, people often underestimate the need to study and develop a more refined relationship to "balance," thinking that because they can stand and move or perform in their field, further study is unnecessary. Wrong again. This is because every movement made in any way is dependent on balance and so an alignment to gravity, which most people underestimate. If balance is off just a little, it will adversely affect the movement and its success. This applies to all movement, from before the beginning to after the end of the movement.

Without perfect balance, you will suffer a lack of stability, mobility, and therefore "power." Changes or adjustments in any activity will be all the more difficult, and you will be severely hampered and vulnerable—a little or a lot, depending on the degree of loss. Care needs to be taken that your balance is always free and independent of any outside influence, or even of your own momentum. Without balance, you cannot be masterful at any physical endeavor, and without mental-emotional or organizational balance in nonphysical interactions, you will also be severely hampered in your efforts.

Of course, the use of what I have created and call "effortless power" depends on using the intrinsic strength of the body. Effortless power uses the unified body aligned perfectly to a task such that the movement compresses this intrinsic force into the ground, creating power without the use of muscular strength. But this is a rather unique and special use of force and is generally unknown, so perhaps not relevant to your efforts. If you imagine that it might be useful, you can find out more in *Zen Body-Being* and other avenues exclusive to my work.

The second part of this distinction is relating effectively to any force that is at hand. Force is basically activity creating an influence tending to change the motion of a body, object, or concept, or the production of motion or stress in a stationary object or concept. Generally, force is activity applied to you, or by you to someone, or something else that influences you or something else in some way, be it physical, conceptual, emotional, or another manner.

When applying a force—using strength, momentum, speed, weight, influence, threat, persuasion, or what have you—you need to remain balanced and unified, and understand the principles and dynamics that maximize the force or utilize the force in the most effective way. You must also know when to use force and when to not, and you must know what kind of force is most appropriate or effective to the circumstance. When dealing with incoming forces—movement, pressure, wind, weight, nonphysical forces, and so on—you need to sensitively feel these forces as they arise so that you can manage them, utilize them, or neutralize them.

One often overlooked, disempowering disposition is to not fully acknowledge the presence, amount, kind, or intent of incoming forces. If the force is seen as a negative, the tendency is either to fear it, to resist it, or to ignore it. Any of these is almost always a bad strategy. To effectively deal with any force, it is best to completely acknowledge and let it be. Even if you don't know how to handle it, you need to accept it as it is to have any chance of relating to it effectively. Being aware of and responding to all occurring forces is essential for being effective in both physical and nonphysical domains.

~

Stay balanced and unified to maximize
applying a force, and to manage, utilize, or
neutralize all influencing forces.

~

Timing

One of the most critical factors in any effective interaction is timing. It is the "when" of an action or speed of an activity. When you take action determines how effective your action will be. You need to feel or sense the proper timing for your actions. Sometimes you need to wait, and sometimes you need to act before you have time to think. It all depends on what's occurring and what's appropriate.

In baseball, for example, if I swing before or after the ball is in the exact location to connect effectively, I will miss or produce a bad result. Timing the swing is essential to success. There are many dimensions and relationships where timing is essential for success and many ways for it to be applied.

For instance, you can make a distinction (albeit non-objective) between someone's intent to begin a process and when he commits to produce a result within this process. It is the timing of your actions that reveals the power of this distinction. The act of intending to create a process is different from the moment when one decides to commit to an action to produce a result within that process. For example, if you are going to sit down in a chair, you begin the process by walking over to the chair, turning and bending your body to begin to sit. This is engaging in a process to sit. At some point, you will actually sit on the chair, and this is the actual act of sitting.

As I've demonstrated many times, timing makes all the difference in outcome. Using the above example of sitting, if at any time in the earlier part of the process I pull the chair away, you will not sit because you relate to your perceptions and will act accordingly. However, at some point you will enter the stage in the process in which you are "sitting" down. This is the commitment to produce the result called sitting—letting your body rest on the chair. If at this moment, I pull the chair away, you will fall on the ground. You will have no choice in the matter, since you have already sent the signals or impulse to the body to "sit," and so it will. Even if you are watching the chair being pulled away from underneath you as you sit, you will fall if you enter the "sit" part of the process when there is no chair. My job is to sense the moment when you intend to sit, just before you actually do it. In order to sit, you must sit. The timing of my actions in relation to your process is what makes the difference. (If you'd like to see this in action search "Peter Ralston: Martial Arts Timing" on Youtube. The video was posted by Cheng Hsin, my school.)

The basic principle of timing, of course, applies to any process or interaction. If you time your actions to occur in the part of a process in which they will be most effective, you can be incredibly effective in any interaction. If you develop the distinction of timing into a constant feeling-sense of when your actions will be most appropriate and effective, you can constantly be doing the right thing at the right time.

~

Know when to act, and when to wait.

~

NON-OBJECTIVE DISTINCTIONS

The non-objective realm of your experience includes such intangible aspects as thinking, feeling, and perception. Even your understanding and feeling-sense of all the objective distinctions above occur in the non-objective domain. Also, in any interaction with people, your decisions, impulses, and plans will relate not just to the other's behavior or actions, but to what you discern is going on in the other's mind.

Furthermore, what's going on in your own mind entirely determines your relationship to any activity. It is where you interpret things and where your decisions are made. Your task here is to clarify these non-objective distinctions in your own experience—what they are, how they contribute to the effectiveness of your actions, and how they can be improved and changed so you can relate appropriately to what's occurring. First, let's briefly look at five major elements that comprise much of your non-objective experience:

1. Perception
2. Interpretation
3. Strategy
4. State
5. Impulse

Simply put, "perception" provides the mere awareness or encounter of something. It only provides the basic function that tells you something is there; otherwise, it is wide open in terms of possibilities relative to the thing or event encountered. "Interpretation" allows for anything you perceive to become useful. Here, it is defined as "that" in your experience, which creates for you a particular relationship to what's encountered. The frequently overlooked problem with interpretation is that it can be wrong. Regardless of its accuracy, interpretation is never the same as whatever is encountered; it is an interpretation of what's encountered. Although this is a necessary activity, if your interpretation is off it will stand in the way of effective interaction. The power of interpretation and imagination provides the ability to establish a "strategy." This is where a plan of action is formulated that you think will accomplish your objectives.

One of the most overlooked elements of experience is the "state" of mind you are in. Your state of mind often lives as if in the background of your experience, and as a distinction it is often swallowed up by your many internal activities. Your state will influence your interpretations as well as your decisions about what actions to take. When you intend to act on a plan in some way, an "impulse" is generated that motivates a particular action, or series of actions, related to your plan—all to manifest your strategy in this moment of interaction.

Now, expanding on these elements, I'll add a couple more distinctions and go into more detail. These components make up your experience of any activity and are occurring from moment to moment in any interaction you participate in. Knowing how your mind works in this largely overlooked and automatic process allows you to change your experience when necessary, and to fine tune or alter your perceptions and actions to better meet the demands of your field of mastery.

SEVEN NON-OBJECTIVE COMPONENTS

In every moment, your experience of an interaction is made up of at least the following distinctions, whether you are aware of making them or not. Your ability or skill is largely dependent upon the degree of accuracy and appropriateness when making these distinctions:

1. Perception
2. Interpretation
3. State
4. Extrapolation
5. Strategy
6. Impulse
7. Interpretation of the Other's Non-Objective Components

With these distinctions, because they may seem far too abstract to be immediately useful, the first thing to do is grasp them intellectually and then isolate each in your experience. Once you can do that, then you'll need to work on recognizing them in your field as you interact.

This will interfere with your normal capacities for a while, so don't expect success right off. But if you're going to change your experience to allow access to mastery, it's best to break down and disengage what you have been doing that doesn't fully work, then re-create it so that it does. After becoming familiar with these distinctions and refining them in your experience, you'll then need to put them all together into one sophisticated feeling-sense. We'll look into how to do that after working through each of these components. Don't worry. We are more than halfway through laying the groundwork for success.

Perception

The "perception" of anything is the basis from which it is known at all. Greater attention on what and how you perceive whatever is there is essential to relate to it more effectively. However, as I have mentioned, perception itself doesn't provide the necessary information required to take appropriate action. So why make this distinction?

The power of grasping the distinction of perception itself, without it being mixed with other elements such as interpretation and extrapolation, is that it provides an experience of more open possibilities. Experiencing this distinction allows for the recognition that what you are interpreting may not be all that is there or even an accurate reflection of what is there. This experience allows you to create alternative perspectives and discover something overlooked or unseen, including errors on your part.

Because you are open to error and correction, you are empowered to grasp what is arising in each moment. Also, you're perceptive-experience is kept fresh by allowing your interpretation to be created newly in every moment. In this way, new information gets into your experience as soon as it arises, rather than being muffled or obscured by past interpretations forcing themselves onto the present—which is a common occurrence. With such openness, you are free to sense the smallest—and what might otherwise be interpreted as insignificant—shift in circumstance, as well as be empowered to re-interpret any interpretation that has been made in error or doesn't provide an appropriate experience that leads to mastery.

■   Perception Exercise   ■

Recall a relatively recent activity at which you were unsuccessful. Go over it in your mind and notice what was going on for you during the engagement. How did you see it? What emotions or other reactions did you have?

How did you assess your performance? What did you think or believe about whatever it was you were interacting with? Try to get a sense of the full "experience" you had in as much detail as you can—your interpretation of the situation, including whatever occurred for you internally and every judgment you had.

Now begin to look at this same event but subtract out all judgments until you can perceive what's there without any judgment, good or bad. Take away all of your reactions to it, and then your assessments about how you did and so on. Strip away all that is not just the presence of what occurred. Recall what actually took place without bias, passion, or prejudice. Take your time.

Once you've accomplished this, perceive the engagement again as it was, and ask yourself: What other ways could you have perceived it? How could you have held what was happening differently and perhaps more effectively? What experience could you have generated in relationship to this event that would be very different from what you did and perhaps much more effective? Be creative.

This kind of shift in experience is the power and freedom offered by grasping the root function of perception.

∽

Creatively question your perceptions, and stay
open to what may be unnoticed.

∽

Interpretation

"Interpretation" is the automatic and speedy mental activity of assessing and categorizing what things are and associating them with your past as well as your assumptions and beliefs. In this process, you also automatically relate everything to yourself and your needs. Although interpretation is necessary in order to relate what you perceive to your goals or objectives, it also often has some inherent dangers and possible errors that will produce ineffectiveness.

Interpretation gives you necessary information about what is happening. However, much of what you mistake for accurate interpretation is actually extrapolation and speculation combined with a bias born from your own desires and fears as well as other reactions or projections that influence this interpretation. Therefore, the distinction between accurate, reflective, and effective interpretation, and all of the self-referencing reactions piled on top of that—thus reducing effectiveness—is a vital distinction to make. Your interpretation must be freed from all that is not accurately representing what's there so that this moment can be seen *as* this moment. By becoming experientially clear on these first two distinctions—perception and interpretation—this ability to see and understand clearly is possible.

Your interpretation will be assessed from past associations but needs to be determined relative your current objectives. If your interpretation is burdened by your own mental and emotional reactions and projections, you can't relate to what's actually there—which, recall, is necessary for effective interaction. Without being conscious of this, or what it means and how it works, many people make regular and unseen errors in their interpretation of things, making them less effective.

By stripping down what is interpreted to its simplest form, freeing it as much as possible from being related to yourself—and instead relating it solely to your objectives—you will eliminate such influences as approval or disapproval, negative or positive charge, judgments, fears, desires, associations, expectations, beliefs, assumptions, opinions, and so on. In this way, you can make more effective interpretations. Your goal is to clearly perceive all that is there, and then interpret it solely in relation to your objectives and purpose, without relating it to your personal needs.

⁓

Interpretation should accurately represent
what's there, and not be weighed down
with personal stuff.

⁓

State

The distinction of "state" is a highly overlooked one. It doesn't fit neatly into the linear progression that the other elements do; it is ongoing and changing throughout. One's mental and emotional state, or state of mind, before and throughout an interaction or event is crucial to your success. Usually, your state is part of your background experience, but it is useful to bring it to the fore and put attention on it, since controlling and creating your state and perspective is probably the most important aspect for achieving mastery.

"State" is the particular condition of mind that someone is in at a specific time. Your state encompasses your frame of mind, mood, perspective, emotional disposition, clarity of thought, and so on. It is the context that holds your internal activities. Most of the time your mental-emotional state is circumstantially derived and so it seems as if it's caused by the environment.

Assuming, however, that your mood, emotions, and state of mind are produced by circumstance makes it seem that you really have no choice in the matter, and so you overlook it as something you can change or control. But just like your interpretations, your state shouldn't be determined by an automatic, self-referencing mechanism that produces reactivity, perspective, and attitudes by mindlessly relating what you encounter to your personal needs and agenda.

We do see some notion that our state can be managed or changed, however, in such undertakings as meditation, gardening, or jogging. The shift in state is very probably why you might do such things. When you meditate you actually are setting out to change your state. In so doing, your thoughts and feelings and perspective also tend to change. People generally acknowledge that this is possible and yet still feel as if they have to take up a practice or an activity to achieve it. Consider that you can change your state just because you change your state.

To pursue mastery, it is mandatory that you master your state so it relates appropriately to the task at hand. Because you need to relate to the current activity, one aspect of any state you create should be *presence*—in other words, being present and aware in each moment. Other states that are often also useful are being calm, clear, sensitive, sometimes detached, and sometimes empathetic, but without entanglement. Whatever states you adopt must be generated to fit the occasion.

You can create states that are accepting, inclusive, open, responsive, focused, enthusiastic, attentive, and on and on. On the other hand, you could be grumpy, closed off, ignorant, belligerent, reactive, bored, distracted, and so on. These latter states are not created on purpose but are the result of the effect circumstance has on you due to personal programming. The possible states on the first list are also almost always generated from circumstance, and so in this way you will remain subject to reactive states rather than creative ones.

The reason this is usually the case is that people often don't grasp or experience that they can create their state. You are probably wed to the assumption that your state is caused by circumstance. Why this appears to seamlessly be the case is a long story best fleshed out in my consciousness trilogy, starting with *The Book of Not Knowing*. In brief: because your mind automatically relates everything encountered to your self-experience, your state is also determined by that activity. The idea that you could change your state rarely occurs except in such activities as meditating to achieve a desired state, or trying to think positively, or trying to calm down, or in similar activities—but only if such possibilities are available for you in your world.

Simply creating a state, as if out of thin air, is not generally an accepted idea. I'd like to introduce it as a necessary one. Mastery demands you not be "at the effect" of circumstance but appropriate to it. If you are in a state that doesn't serve your objectives, it needs to change. What can you imagine as best-case states for you to be in and act from that are appropriate for your field of mastery? States include more than emotion, but emotions may be the most obvious element. To assist in learning to master emotions and change states, start with an exercise I have given my apprentices.

■   Creating Emotions and States Exercise   ■

Start by paying attention to your emotions throughout the day. Whenever you notice you have an emotion going on, first feel it and allow it to be there, but give it no meaning or motivating power. Allow it to be there "for-itself," so to speak—which is similar to the exercise you did on perception.

Once you are able to do this relatively easily and consistently with any emotion, then move on to changing the emotion. Several times a day, practice instantly changing any emotion you have to several others. When you notice you have an emotion, say anger for example, let it be, and then change it completely, and feel a different emotion instead. Often, at this point, people seem baffled by how to do that until they realize they can just do it.

At first, people usually think they have to imagine some circumstance that would elicit that emotion. For instance, if they are trying to feel love, they might focus on a loved one in their imagination. Perhaps as a warm-up this can be useful, but no imagined circumstance is necessary. If you want to feel love, simply feel love. Like magic! Just create it, and make it real.

Once you can do this, practice rather rapidly changing any emotion to three or four other emotions or feeling-states on the spot. For example, you might change your anger to love, fear, enthusiasm, and then sadness.

You can create any emotion or feeling-state. Simply bring it to life and stay with it until it feels real to you. You can adopt joy, contempt, grief, shame, courage, lust, anxiety, hope, passion, calm, boredom, satisfaction, or any other feeling-state. The trick is to learn to "master" emotions by being able to create them or change them at will. Of course, in order to do this, you have to pull your self-concerns out of the picture, and you may need to detach from intimate issues you feel unwilling to give up in your personal life. Once you can change emotions at will, your relationship to emotions should change, and you'll certainly experience being more responsible for their existence.

It might take some time and effort for you to develop this kind of ability. Perhaps some feeling-states will come to you easily, while others may require more attention until they become easy to adopt. Once you have developed this grounded ability, move on to doing the same exercise with changing your state. Change your perspective or mood, your sense of being in the world, your thinking, attitudes, and so on. It doesn't matter what you change into, just that you change several times in relatively quick succession. Make sure you aren't just pretending but are actually adopting that new state. As you become skilled at this, imagine other possible states that you, or perhaps anyone, have never experienced, and create them. Make them feel real.

When you can do that with some capacity, begin to consider what state or states would be powerful in relation to your endeavor. Also consider what states might be useful to particular kinds of engagements likely to occur in your field. Don't limit yourself to past states you've experienced, but consider that you can create, as if by magic, any new state—almost like a superpower—that you think may empower your efforts in a particular endeavor. Over time, depending on your field, you can develop several different states and principles (which also demand a commensurate state in order to be effective) that are effective in specific situations, domains, or activities. When that happens, you are much closer to mastery.

Beyond refining all of these non-objective distinctions, adopting an appropriate state will likely be your most valuable asset for mastery. Now, moving back to the more linear progression of these components, you'll find that your perception and interpretation of the situation is joined by another function, extrapolation.

～

Master your state of mind, and create the best
state for the job at hand.

～

Extrapolation

"Extrapolation" is a constant part of your interpretation. Extrapolation is having a concept of what will occur in the future drawn from the patterns seen in what has occurred so far. Extrapolation is necessary in order to recognize possible outcomes. It allows you to take action toward a future process. For example, if I see you swing your arm to throw a ball in my direction, I will instantly extrapolate out the rest of the process, coming to the conclusion that the ball will take a certain path and come down at a particular location. From this extrapolation, I will begin moving my body to the place the ball will land so I can catch it. This is also true and active in business activities, interpersonal relating, and so on.

As valuable as this process is, there are still dangers. Most people don't make the distinction between what is occurring now and their extrapolation of where it is going. For instance, notice right now that your attention is not on simply what you are reading but on where it is going. The fundamental problem with extrapolation is that it is usually held as something that is occurring, when in reality it is only a concept of the future, and at best suggests a likely probability. If in reading or listening, for example, you draw a conclusion about where the communication is going—and likely one that fits your beliefs—you may well miss what is being said that doesn't match your extrapolation. Much of what hampers people's ability to interact in spontaneously occurring events is their attachment to extrapolations. Any extrapolation can be wrong.

In some domains and segments of time, extrapolations can be counted on. For instance, when you pick up a foot to take a step, your foot will and must come down, and usually in very predictable ways. In the case of the thrown ball, if your assessment is accurate, the ball will probably do what you predict, but even then a sudden wind or other influence might change its trajectory. In the physical and social domains, any simple act is often quite predicable if your interpretation and extrapolations are accurate. But in any interaction, there is always the next moment, and things can change.

People change their minds or strategies, or changes in circumstance can throw a monkey wrench into the works, and so on. The future is unknown, and events can change and often do. When you fixate on an extrapolation, holding it as an occurring fact rather than a concept of the future—an educated guess—you tend to miss any changes that occur in the activity until it's too late to relate to them appropriately. Clarifying this distinction in your experience, you can train yourself to be open to changes and be able to reassess unfolding events in an instant.

～

Keep all extrapolations up to date.

～

Strategy

Within these non-objective distinctions, four are about receiving information needed to act effectively—perception, interpretation, extrapolation, and knowing the other's experience (when appropriate). Three are about relating to this information—state, strategy, and impulse. Whatever plan or "strategy" you come up with to reach your objective will have perhaps the greatest impact on your success or lack of it. The "what to do," once you have accurate data, is what decides whether or not you are successful.

Whatever your objective is, you should immediately compare it to what's occurring. This provides a map showing where you're at circumstantially in the moment compared to where you want to go. From this observation, a strategy or plan for action can be assessed, providing an idea of what needs to occur to reach your goals.

As a simple example, let's say I want to catch a turtle walking away from me on the beach. I assess he is 100 feet away and moving at a slow speed, and calculate that I will have to cover about 110 feet to get to him at the speed he's going if I jog at a certain pace. This outlines a very simple strategy for action to attain my goal. If I see that he speeds up, I may have to change my plans, because now new data has been introduced.

In a far more complex interaction, such as a martial contest, there is much more to assess in what's occurring from moment to moment. There are also many more possible outcomes, creating the need for fast problem solving and being able to generate strategies for each possibility. Such an interaction has many interrelating elements and involves rapidly changing circumstances, so the demands for change and intelligent creativity become even more acute.

For example, if you want to throw me down, what you see in the immediate relationship between our two bodies has a great deal to do with what you glean as your opportunities for throwing me down. This demands considerations and distinctions regarding what you think it takes to throw somebody. But if you don't throw people down much, you won't perceive a great deal that I would. Do you see the need for extra distinctions to be effective with your effort? Because I will be making more distinctions than you, I will know where your feet are, feel your resistance and balance, sense your intentions, notice the structure of your body, consider your immediate actions, discern your strategy, and consider myriad other factors that have to do with throwing.

If my objective were something other than to throw you—perhaps to support you in an environmental project we're working on together—I might never have noticed any of these things, and they would not have appeared in my interpretation and evaluation. Instead, many other distinctions would have appeared. This is how your objective influences interpretation.

In relation to my concern for throwing you, I will design a strategy for action. Perhaps I decide to rock your body slightly off balance, and then, as you step to keep your balance, I change the direction of applied force at precisely the right time and angle so that you are caught critically off balance, are unable to adjust adequately, and thus fall down. From this strategic idea, the first thing I see is whether or not, and how, I can rock you off balance. This is how strategy influences interpretation.

In such a case, you can see all this goes on at lightning speed, and any change in my assessment of circumstances demands an immediate change in plans. Many different strategies can be created to realize an objective. As I mentioned earlier, it is imperative that you do not make the objective subservient to the strategy, which frequently happens.

People often fall into the trap of making their strategy the objective. The main problem with this is that the strategy may not work. Even if it does work for a time, or has the possibility of working for a time, it is quite possible, and even likely, that circumstances will change so that the strategy is no longer effective. When, out of an ignorance regarding the nature of how these things work, you allow the strategy to displace the objective—by thinking they are the same thing, or that the strategy will necessarily produce the desired results—you may well be left with an ineffective strategy without the possibility of creating something new. This is unnecessary.

Objectives are related to a particular endeavor and need to be consistent with your purpose as well as accomplish your desired results. The purpose, however, is not restricted to any objective, strategy, or even field. It can be accomplished in all sorts of ways. For example, perhaps my purpose in pursuing mastery in the fighting arts is to improve my ability to handle difficult circumstances so that I will experience a greater sense of effectiveness, confidence, and personal power in my life. You can see that the purpose may be fulfilled by realizing many different objectives. All that needs to take place is that I feel empowered to handle difficult circumstances. As a matter of fact, I could change my field from fighting to any other field where I am empowered with a greater ability to handle difficult circumstances—I might open a business, take up a sport, get married, or engage in any endeavor where I can learn and develop in relation to my purpose.

The "purpose" is why you take something on. The "field" is the activity you use to pursue your purpose. Within this field will be particular activities you'll engage, and within these activities you will create far-reaching as well as immediate "objectives" to achieve the results you think are necessary for mastery.

A "goal" simply has to promise to move the interaction toward your objective. Yet it must become a particular goal requiring specific action, or it won't work. Although specific actions and goals must take place, in any given moment the goal or action may need to change in order to be appropriate. If any action, goal, or objective is ever discovered to be inappropriate or off purpose, it should be replaced by one that is on purpose. Any plan must always be pliable and open to change.

In order to be successful, you have to know what success is and be able to recognize it when it occurs, even if it occurs in a form that you didn't envision when first imagining how success might look. The moment you pin the objective down to one plan of action or method of attainment, you are severely hampered in getting the job done. With this restriction, you can only try harder, be more clever, or do better at what you're already doing—and those are not the best strategies for success.

You are also likely to have hidden personal objectives that influence your actions. If you have some unstated objective, such as looking good, taking revenge, or proving you're not worthless, you will devote much of your energy to these goals, and not be focused on realizing pertinent objectives. Burdening your efforts with such nonrelated personal objectives makes what you're doing ineffective. If your strategy for action is not based on solid ground and on an accurate or workable interpretation of the occurring event, then simply trying harder will not work. You will be ineffective and not know why.

Being clear about your objective is the first step toward avoiding this mistake. Understanding that the plan serves the objective or goal, and not vice versa, helps you remain open to change and correction. In this way, the objective can mold and design the strategy, altering it from moment to moment as is appropriate. The task here is to see that your objectives determine your strategies. If you can improve and clarify this distinction in your experience, you will be empowered to avoid certain confusion, mistakes, and traps, and have a much greater capacity to be effective.

■   Strategy Exercise   ■

Bring to mind the field you are trying to master. What plans do you typically make and undertake? Can you find similarities in your strategies? Consider in what ways you might be limiting yourself or being myopic. What patterns, methods, or dispositions do you tend to repeat?

See if you can discover hidden agendas—personal objectives you're trying to accomplish for yourself or your self-image, or things you are trying to cover up, ignore, or prove. Can you find these in any way influencing your strategies or actions in your endeavor?

Now, imagine freeing your approach and plans from any hidden agenda or personal influence, and look at how this changes what you would create as a strategy.

Look again at your arena and view it cleanly and without personal bias. What states and strategies do you think would be most appropriate? See if you can come up with new strategies. Don't hold back, but look in unexpected places and entertain uncommon methods. Even if these don't pan out, it is good to exercise your brain in this way, and you may well open a door to something that works you'd previously overlooked.

Once you've exercised your imagination, consider strategies that would pretty much guarantee mastery. These would need to include the realities of your field, as well as principles that really work. In some arenas, plans have to be created on the spot as actions unfold. But the arena itself has parameters and predictable aspects to it, and so you can create many different plans beforehand, such as, "if they do this, I could do that," or, "if this happens, such and such a response would be appropriate," and so on. This prepares you to meet the challenges that are likely to arise.

～

Never make the strategy master over the
objective. The strategy should always serve the
objective, and change the moment it doesn't.

～

Impulse

Once perception, interpretation, state, extrapolation, and strategy take place—and remember, all these can seem to occur at light speed—you will make a decision as to what action to take or not to take. This decision does not have to be intellectual or a deliberation; it can be almost instantaneously arising. Once a decision is made—whether after considered deliberation, or arising suddenly and constantly changing—this decision will take the form of an intent, and this intent immediately creates an "impulse" to produce an action.

The feeling-distinction of impulse is the activity that creates action or any shift of mind within your internal state. It is what links your *intention* to *action*. Whatever happens, whatever action you take, is a result of an impulse that generates that action. It bridges the gap between your non-objective activities and your physical actions.

Impulse is always a feeling of some kind, because that is what generates action. Study any action you take and notice it arises via a feeling-sense that produces the action. In some cases, it may seem subtle or difficult to ascertain, such as when you speak or change your internal state. Still, you should be able to find the feeling-impulse that generates action. It is often almost indistinguishable from the action itself.

Raise your hand. Go ahead, lift your arm and hand up. Now, how did you do that? What happened that made your hand go up? Do it a few times and study it. What occurs so that your hand moves? Obviously, you have the thought and intent to do it. This can go almost unnoticed, can't it? But it still occurs. And this intent creates an impulse that is the lifting of the hand. It is not something that happens independent of the lifting itself. It is what moves the arm and hand. Can you experience this?

If you have some challenge with this, close your eyes and move your arm. How do you know the arm moved when you can't see it? You feel it, don't you? That feeling is not just the sensation of the air passing over your moving skin, it is the feeling-impulse that moves your arm and also tells you what it is doing. It is the same for all actions. This is quite a simple example and in this case, rarely does anything get in the way. But in other cases, the bridge between impulse and action can get clogged with inappropriate impulses that don't relate effectively to what's occurring.

As with other distinctions, it's important to distinguish between an impulse that is on purpose, arising to serve appropriate action, and all the other impulses that arise as reactions to self-referencing personal needs, fears, and agendas. The latter impulses are not effective and should be let go when participating in your field. Obviously, in any immediately demanding interaction you also need for your intent and action to occur without delay and not be passed through unnecessary filters or processes. So it's important that your impulses be quickly responsive and not clogged with baggage.

Why are personal concerns not appropriate to effective relating? An interaction is about two or more, not one. When you're trying to have your individual or personal needs or desires met, or are trapped by your fears, or are focused exclusively on trying to manipulate the world or other(s) to serve your individual concerns, you are in the wrong frame of mind for effectively interacting with others or objects that have nothing to do with your personal agenda.

A self-agenda is really about how any interaction can ease your own suffering. This might take the form of trying to be liked, feel safe, get revenge, prove your worth, obtain comfort or wealth, or do whatever else drives you to pursue some personal resolution. But these kinds of attainments relate to personal concerns, not to your endeavor's objectives. Therefore, to be masterful, your impulses must relate to what's occurring independent of your personal agenda.

For mastery, you need to generate new and effective impulses that are free of personal reactivity and drives, because these reactions don't really relate to the occurring event or to your objective. Instead, you must create impulses that relate solely to the objective, intending for it to come to pass while remaining aware of what's occurring in present time. This is important to understand. People often focus on the result while engaged in a process to bring it about. That's not what I'm talking about here; it is a mistake and reduces effectiveness by drawing attention (and thus action) away from what's occurring or what needs to be occurring now.

Movement, applying force, response, adjustment, realignment, speaking, or any other activity within the body-mind occurs through impulse. Impulse generates action and so is how a strategy is brought into reality. Yet if your impulses are circumstantially derived and merely reactions to stimuli, this will tend to block an accurate experience of and appropriate response to what's there, and so your actions will be less effective.

On the other hand, if you not only work hard to press your perceptive-interpretation to accurately reflect the current condition, but go further to allow the possibility of creating impulses that aren't reactive, you can be successful. This will allow you to create a state or perspective that produces impulses—and so actions—free of reactivity and not limited to the effects of circumstance. Using only familiar impulses may not be enough to get the job done. You also have to be creative and reach for new impulses. In this way, if you are successful, you can essentially use states and impulses as if to effectively "will" results into place.

To approach this ability, you need to go beyond searching through your known world of impulses, and instead create a new perspective where you can invent impulses you've never experienced before. Of course, even doing this can go awry if your impulse isn't appropriate to what's occurring. So you need to have a way to know if any created perspective or impulse is appropriate—in other words, if it would produce the desired outcome.

This "creative possibility" can be formed in any number of ways. A feeling-state and unusual feeling-impulses can be created in a fashion that you intuit will be effective for the interaction, even if you can find no logical reason why it should. This frees you to concentrate on what you want to have arise, without intellectually worrying about or wasting time on how that arising needs to occur. You can effectively "feel" success into existence.

This is not to suggest that merely willing something to come to pass will make it happen, or that positive thinking is in any way enough. It does, however, suggest that you can develop a new ability, generating a feeling-intent that serves to bring about your desired outcome. Such an ability requires a new kind of intelligence that is inclusive and insightful—founded on a great deal of experiential training and learning—where you can leap past pedestrian thought processes and instead sense what state or impulse needs to be created, without it being based on past patterns, the need to figure it out, or your personal concerns.

The idea of "willing" the outcome to come about as if by magic, albeit through committed action, is both unconventional and conventional. Its conventionality can be found in the idea that stubborn determination is enough to make something happen, or the idea that wishful thinking will bring something about, or the idea that some outcome is destined or deserved, and in other such notions. None of these are what I'm recommending nor are they useful. What's being recommended is actually unconventional.

It involves new abilities, carefully crafted states, effective principles, creative intuitive-intelligence, and committed action. Altogether, these allow an open and creative feeling relationship to the task, bringing in new possibilities—not always visible—that influence the process. This approach can have a greater impact on producing success than is generally thought possible. Such inventive creativity is closely linked to changing your state. (For a deeper look into how this is so, again study the section "Practice, Principle, Being" (p. 35), and consider how much the absorption and alignment with a principle can contribute to your experience and so your effectiveness.

You've probably heard of, and have likely experienced, times when mind and action, intent and outcome, came together in a sublime way. Consider the baseball player at bat, who, in the middle of a swing *knows* that this one will be a home run—and this is confirmed as the bat cracks the ball with that perfect sound. Consider the boxer, who, against all odds, wills himself to beat an unbeatable opponent by doing all the right things in each moment throughout the fight. When a gymnast like Nadia Comăneci flies through a routine, bringing in the first perfect 10, there is no room for thought or doubt or anything but the immediate perfection of movement.

I'm sure you have experienced skill doing certain tasks, and know that when you are good at something there is a "feeling" you produce that is inherent in the action that will make it work out. Now, imagine that instead of finding this feeling through lots of repetition, you search for and create it through sensing what it is by applying concentration and insight. Also imagine you can create other feeling-states and impulses in relation to whatever is needed at the time. Clearly, controlling the mind and being wed to appropriate feeling-impulses are necessary for mastery to unfold.

Since all of the above distinctions should be made as a feeling-sense, the entire scope of intelligence that they provide is instantly available to your intent. This intent immediately produces feeling-impulses that will generate both internal activity and objective action. From here, your actions can be channeled instantly and appropriately, without intellect, reactivity, or secondary processes getting in the way.

■   Intent and Impulse Exercise   ■

Dwell on a recent interaction you experienced within your field. In hindsight, work to separate out all of your personal agenda impulses and quirks from the feeling-state and impulse control needed to master your field. What are you left with when you do that?

What kinds of motivating impulses, and thus actions, do you think would serve you in being more effective? Focus on one action and isolate what you think is the proper intent and impulse that would make that action a success. Act it out in your mind, feeling the impulse and generating the action, and then observe, as best you can, what comes about because of it. If you sense it will miss the mark or can be improved, make adjustments and try again. Do this until you feel like you can create an appropriate impulse that produces a masterful result. Now combine all of the unfolding actions you imagine are necessary for success in a segment of your endeavor and do the same thing, willing a string of impulses to be seamless and effective.

Next, imagine inventing new impulses and states that you've never experienced before, and in your mind, try them out in an imagined scenario. Seek out states and feeling-impulses that you think would create mastery in your endeavor, even though it might seem this is done as if by magic. Don't restrict yourself.

When you think you've found some feeling-states or impulses that might work, try them out in a real situation and see what occurs. If you aren't successful at generating these feeling-states and actions then keep repeating the attempt until you are. If you can generate them but they don't produce the results that you imagined, then use the feedback from the attempt and make adjustments and try again. If the feedback suggests you are on the wrong track, go back to the drawing board and create a whole new set of feeling-states and try again. Do this until you have success.

~

Wed all impulses to the current event, and allow
your impulses to be creative.

~

Interpretation of the Other's
Non-Objective Components

In any endeavor involving others—and most fields of mastery involve others in some way, either directly or indirectly—this is one of the most important distinctions to be made. It's actually a conglomerate of distinctions. If you are directly interacting with another or others, you need to constantly be aware of the experience that the other person or persons are having. What is *their* perception, interpretation, extrapolation, state, objective, strategy, and intent?

In your perception-interpretation you always have some idea as to what these are, yet often neglect to look into them deeply, demand accuracy, or remain current. You end up relating to a superficial, and often past or biased, interpretation of what others are really up to. In any interaction, your degree of accuracy in reading another's intent and strategy, and in being aware of his or her impulses and actions, will determine the outcome of the interaction. This is true for both physical and nonphysical interactions. Once you are clear and trained in the first six distinctions regarding your own experience, most of your attention should be on the other's experience—and if no other is in the picture, then on the object or circumstance.

Asking questions—such as, "What is she seeing? What is she thinking? What is she trying to do? What is her strategy?"—draws your attention to the experience the other is having of the interaction. This experience will always be different from your own. You must be open to the fact that another's experience will not be the same as yours, and may be founded on a radically different framework of mind and value systems than yours, and so may be a completely foreign experience to you.

The other's point of view will necessarily be different from yours. This is so if for no other reason than he is looking at and relating to you and you are not. In a competitive interaction, his objectives will be contrary to yours. For example, if you're playing a game, the other person wants to win the game as do you, which requires that he prevent you from doing so. His objectives will also quite likely be different in nature than yours. He may not have the same purpose in mind for the interaction, and he may have a different system by which to evaluate the process. So, what is good, bad, or insignificant to him may not be the same as what is so for you. These things must be taken into account and the reality sought out.

When I have people do exercises or games with various partners, I frequently ask them to notice that the interaction with each person is different from every one of the others. I point out that this is not only a function of having different physical attributes. The most important aspect is that they're all actually playing a different game.

People think that because everyone has the same rules for a game or exercise, they must be doing the same thing, just better or worse. This isn't the case. The overlooked element is that they are actually not playing the same game. Different people will hear the rules differently, attribute more significance to some areas and less to others, assess the nature of winning consistent with their personal belief systems, have hidden agendas, and so on. So, the activity any person is doing won't be the same as whatever the other person is doing.

Having in your experience the context and content that make up the other's experience is, perhaps, the most important aspect of any relationship that works out well. It is the other's actions that you need to interact with, and it is his experience that determines his actions. In some arenas, such as golf, one is mostly playing against oneself, though others are also involved. In other arenas, like fighting or business, others are the main feature, and success entirely depends on how you relate to them.

Because most people don't put enough attention on a clear and unbiased experience of what's so for the other, they are short-changed in their ability to interact effectively. Once made, however, a refined distinction of another's experience represents a fundamentally new dimension in your experience. Suddenly, a fresh depth and domain of experience emerges, out of which a greater effectiveness arises quite naturally.

~

Develop a refined and accurate feeling-sense of
the other's experience in each moment.

~

All of the objective and non-objective distinctions mentioned above already occur in some form for everyone, yet they are usually all mushed together in an experience that is simplistic and insensitive as well as confused with personal agendas that get in the way. When these distinctions are made, they are frequently made very poorly and without a great deal of clarity or experiential understanding of their nature and significance. For mastery to occur, that needs to change.

I suspect that at this point you may feel overwhelmed by the plethora of information. I recommend that you go back to the introduction to refresh your memory of what you need to do in order to get all this. To help you bring these distinctions together I offer the following review in an outline form.

A Short Outline of the
Five Objective Distinctions

1. Keep a feeling-connection with the weight, shape, design, and substance of any object.
2. Stay constantly immersed in three-dimensional awareness; feel changes in distance and spatial relations.
3. Know the meaning of each stage of an occurring process, and relate appropriately.
4. Stay unified and balanced to maximize applying a force and to manage all influencing forces.
5. Know when to act and when to wait.

A Short Outline of the
Seven Non-Objective Components

1. Stay open to errors in your perceptions.
2. Interpretation should accurately represent what's there and not be weighed down with personal stuff.
3. Master your state of mind, and create the best state for the circumstance.

4. Keep all extrapolations up to date, and be alert to possible changes.

5. Never make the strategy master over the objective. The strategy should always serve the objective and change the moment it doesn't.

6. Wed all impulses to the current event, and allow your impulses to be creative.

7. Develop a refined and accurate feeling-sense of any other's experience in each moment.

FEELING TRANSLATION

Once each distinction is individually studied and mastered, all distinctions need to be put together and act as a whole in one sophisticated but simple experience. This experience is best honed into a new kind of feeling-sense that includes all of the distinctions needed for mastery.

To accomplish this, every distinction that you make must be translated into something like a feeling, regardless of the perceptive organ from which it originates. You must learn to "feel" with your eyes, ears, nose, brain, and every other part of your body and mind so that when you perceive anything you "feel" all of the implications of its presence. In this way, you can act directly in response to the appearance of any action or situation using a feeling-experience of what's occurring, providing you the necessary information about what to do and how to do it. This kind of development is very important for mastery.

That this occurs as a feeling-sense in no way implies that it is not highly intelligent. As a matter of fact, it is far more intelligent than intellect or emotion or other faculties engaged alone. This translation combines all incoming data, regardless of source, into one feeling-sense so that it can be easily related to your objectives. The sophisticated and complex integration of all these factors into one feeling-sense provides a new depth of intelligence that requires no delay in order to respond.

If your perception appears in some form that must then be translated into action, or put through an intellectual or emotional process before you can respond, then this means an intermediary and slower process must take place. This lengthy process is far too removed from the immediately occurring event for most purposes. You want your actions and impulses to be as "reflective" as possible.

I don't mean that your responses are mechanical or in any way reactive or lack intelligence, but that they are immediate to the event—they "reflect" the event. This occurs like the moonbeam in still water reflects the moon—accurately, and without middleman, process, or delay. The instant the moon changes, so does the reflection. If the "water" is disturbed, however—through reactions, personal concerns, and so on—it will not clearly reflect what's there, and the reflection will be badly distorted. So it is important to keep the mind calm and your feeling-sense free of distortion and dysfunctional baggage.

Some endeavors require an immaculately precise and immediate response, but for those that don't, more time can be taken to respond. In either type of endeavor, the ability to accurately reflect serves to move you closer to mastery. This intelligent feeling-sense allows you to not only have your experience reflect what's occurring but also combines many distinctions into one feeling-awareness, so you have a sophisticated and accurate experiential relationship to each moment of interaction without having to intellectualize or "think" about it. This is a necessary ability to have in physical domains and extremely useful in nonphysical domains.

Notice that you already do this to some degree. When you see a Styrofoam cup tossed your way you will "feel" the cup as it passes through the air and adjust your response accordingly. Contrast this to the feeling you would have if it were a brick tossed to you. Eliminating any fear or other reactions from the feeling reveals how much information you really have in such a feeling-sense. Now imagine refining and applying this same feeling-sense to every aspect of your field. For example, being able to "feel" distance, movement, another's experience, a legal argument, another's intention, this moment of process, your overall strategy compared to what's happening, balance, space, ground, a communication, a piece of art, and so on. Feel whatever constitutes every aspect of your endeavor.

In combat, if I see you move, I will assess a weight shift, pick up an intention, sense a loss of balance, feel the relationship between the two bodies, and make many other feeling-distinctions. If I then had to intellectually assess and command my mind and body to take advantage of these observations, the situation would have already passed. My response would no longer be in relation to the moment but to a past moment of observation.

On the other hand, when my experience contains the reflective and inclusive feeling-sense that I'm describing—if every distinction that I make is received in the form of a sophisticated feeling—then I can respond immediately. Since action arises from a feeling-impulse, these impulses can relate immediately to the feeling-distinctions that are feeding information to the body-mind. They speak the same language, so to speak.

Eventually, as development occurs along these lines, the other's actions or circumstantial activity can actually seem to generate your actions, with very little intellectual deliberation on your part. At this stage, your role appears more like directing the flow of activity to align to a principle rather than deciding what action to take. That's not actually true, and many intelligent decisions are made at light speed, but since the operating principle dominates the relationship, and the objective is always present and related to a feeling-sense of what's happening, such decisions don't have to pass through any additional deliberative thought processes.

Even in fields that don't require immediate response, this sophisticated feeling-sense is essential for mastery. An artist who is a master painter, for example, has very sophisticated feeling-distinctions about all the elements involved in putting paint to canvas. Perhaps even more importantly, he can feel the creation of the art and how to get there. It may take trial and error to find that piece of art, but it is a sophisticated feeling-sense that tells him that the attempt missed the mark and didn't hit home. Yet it also provides feedback to help him find and create this particular piece of art. This feedback itself mostly exists in a feeling-sense domain that is rare and unconventional, allowing the artist to create a masterpiece.

Of course, to reach this stage of reflective, complex, and sophisticated feeling translation and be effective, you must experience whatever information is necessary to direct the processes intelligently. Making the distinctions I've addressed, and turning them into a feeling-sense, should provide much, if not all, of this information. In working to create appropriate action, however, within the domain of feeling, we also need to make a distinction between reaction and response.

REACTION VERSUS RESPONSE

So that we are on the same page about action springing from a feeling-sense, it is important to understand the difference between response and reaction. A response arises from a calm mind and sensitive awareness. It tends to be accurate and emerges from a state of equanimity and balance. It is not blocked or forced but occurs naturally. It is not weighed down with fear, desire, or indecision. Instead, it is directed by a present feeling-intelligence in order to relate to what's occurring. The intent of responsive action is to produce what is needed and appropriate in a given situation.

A reaction, however, is the antithesis of a response, although both are actions in relationship to something perceived. A reaction arises from automatic impulses. It tends to be motivated by such activities as fear, desire, resistance, vulnerability, anger, or other knee-jerk self-protective actions. It occurs as a blind thrashing, acting from an unconscious tendency toward protection, and is contracting in nature. It promotes a withdrawal of sensitivity and relational awareness to act, often in a negative fashion, in an attempt to end the apparent source of danger or dilemma.

There is no real participation in or responsibility for that act, and no sense of what is really appropriate. A reaction is not geared for continuation. It is a one-shot attempt to save oneself. It is often an expression that stems from of a sense of urgency to be protected, unconsciously founded on a feeling of inadequacy to accomplish a task responsibly.

Reactive tendencies are not always violent or sudden, but they always seem to involve a sense of fear and dilemma. They are, by nature, not based on the moment, but emotionally bound to the past and recoiling from the future. Although safety and security are most often motivating factors in a reactive tendency, in some cases the reaction itself may well evoke more suffering and imbalance (therefore danger) than if no action at all had been taken. The relationship between self and situation is often made worse.

When I was fifteen, I was driving a WWII jeep in the mountains of Colorado. I had only just learned how to drive by driving it on the ranch I was working at in the mountains. We had an assignment to set up an outdoor fire pit for dinner for the rich guests of my godfather, John King, the owner of the ranch. This required driving on the highway to get to another location. As I was driving, illegally of course, I was passed by Mel White in his jeep. (Mel was the original owner of the ranch and had been in prison for three years because in a card game another man drew on him—but Mel was faster and shot him. Colorful tale.) Thinking I might be in four-wheel drive, thus slowing me down, I looked down at the gears. When I looked up, the road was turning suddenly to the left and I was about to hit a reflector. I reacted and suddenly swung the car to the left, but went too far and so snapped back to the right, and flipped the jeep.

As I bounced off the pavement and into the ditch I saw the upside-down jeep sliding toward me. Then I passed out. When I awoke, jeep parts were all around, and my first thought was that maybe I could turn the jeep back over and no one would notice. Turned out, I tried and wasn't able to stand, so flipping the jeep wasn't going to happen. Soon, my godfather and astronaut Buzz Aldrin—a few years before he went to the moon—drove by and stopped (astronauts were allowed to stay at the ranch, which was considered a safe place). Buzz helped me out of the ditch. He took me back to the ranch, and we flew in John's plane to a doctor. I was in the back of the plane as my godfather showed Buzz his new "stalling techniques," with my stomach the worse for it. In any case, my reaction on the highway caused an unnecessary accident, whereas a calm response would have been far more appropriate. But I did get to meet Buzz.

When a conflict seems to have been resolved by a reaction, most often it is a postponement, not a resolution, and the real cost has not yet been realized. Of course, sometimes a reaction appears to have saved the day. However, this is the exception and cannot be counted on. Furthermore, we must clearly distinguish between a fast response and a reaction.

The essence of the distinction between these two lies mostly in the state of mind. Responsive action is free from fear and obsessive desire (and I don't mean free from feeling fear or having desire; I mean not bound to, motivated by, or influenced by them) and receptive to the real condition. If the mind and feeling-state are sensitive to but not disrupted by the stimulus that calls for action, then it is responsive. If the stimulus does not call for action, no action is taken. On the other hand, reactions can occur whether action is appropriate for or not.

When we react, our feeling-state is disturbed, the mind is upset, and an unconscious impulse sources the act that is taken. By design, reactions are general, not specific to the immediate situation. They act in opposition to what is perceived. They tend to have a one-size-fits-all relationship to what's occurring.

When thoughts and feelings are nonreactive, calm, and responsive only, then you become natural and remain mentally balanced in the midst of activity. Within responsiveness, your body-being returns continuously to its natural condition, is balanced, and becomes still as soon as activity is not called for. In this way, the body and mind remain intact, whole, relaxed, and always open to appropriate action. You are not recoiling internally, have no wave of resistance, and are not mindlessly taking impulsive actions.

Maintaining this condition of relaxed balance is as delicate as it is effective. On one level, it is like being able to not blink when something flashes toward your eyes. The root of achieving this lies in that urge to react, not in the activity itself. Don't try to stop the act; merely remove the urge, and no act will arise.

Regardless of field, mastery requires appropriate response, not reactivity. Both response and reactivity are functions of how we relate to what's perceived. Since mastery is always about some kind of relationship, to be able to further transform your experience it is also useful to rethink relationship in a more existential way, so you can free it from some of the more commonly shared limiting assumptions.

RETHINKING RELATIONSHIP

For unprecedented learning, it is always useful to create a new and open kind of thinking to counter overlooked assumptions that entrap your interpretations in ineffective ways. Consider that you operate within a framework of beliefs and assumptions that influence every interpretation you make. It is this very framework that yields your current level of effectiveness.

In order to break free from some of the more fundamental assumptions—though the descriptions that follow are by no means a complete list of all possible assumptions—it might be helpful to address a few assertions that can act as a counter to your current framework.

Relationship Is Not an Object

This may seem like a silly thing to say, but consider it more deeply. When you think of the existence of something, you probably think in terms of an object—and if not an actual object, then something held as if it were an object.

For example, when you think of God, whether you believe in God or not, without thinking about it you probably imagine God as some kind of divine person—ergo object—that exists somewhere. Yet if you consider the matter, you will realize that would be impossible. God couldn't possibly be a person or an object or even located somewhere if the attributes assigned were true—creator of existence, omnipresent, infinite, and so on. It is even hard not to refer to God as "him." This same sloppy thinking and tendency shows up in many places in our reality. It is within this assumption that everything is an "object" you'll probably search for mastery. In other words, without thinking you will imagine or assume that mastery is somehow a "thing," an object to attain, even though it isn't.

You cannot create something from something. Objects do not create; they "exist." Notice that you don't have a direct experience of creating the object that you are, and you also have no direct consciousness of how any object comes to exist. Consequently, you can't make objects appear out of thin air, and so if ability were an object you'd have no way to create ability.

In other words, rearranging stuff into a new form is not the creation of objective existence. Sometimes people think they are being creative by taking what already exists and moving it around, but this isn't real creativity. Creativity demands that something comes to exist that previously didn't exist. Ability, however, is not an object. Therefore, there is no "thing" that is created. Ability is created only through how you *relate* to what is occurring. It is created by the distinctions you make and the actions you take. In this way, when you create mastery something comes to exist that didn't exist before you created it, and it is not an object of any kind.

When you unknowingly hold that relationship is somehow an

object—in other words, that you "have" a relationship, whether with a mate, parent, friend, enemy, or someone else—you stand on many assumptions that just aren't true, even if it seems like they are. Without thinking, you'll assume that the relationship exists independent of your relating. It doesn't. For example, you might say and think you are in a "bad" relationship, that there is nothing you can do about it because the relationship itself is somehow just a bad one. This is holding your relating as if it were somehow some "thing," independent from the actions you take.

When something is held as if it's some kind of object, you'll assume that it has certain characteristics and exists in a particular way, and so must follow historical patterns. But think about it. If you relate (think, feel, act, respond) and perceive another or an object or an idea in a completely different manner, it wouldn't have the same characteristics, would it? How you relate to what's there is a function of you, a function that is, in fact, wide open. Obviously, changing how you relate is necessary in order to create mastery.

Freedom from the assumption that relationships are objects is useful because there is nothing that exists like an object that is mastery; you can't attain mastery by obtaining some mysterious power or non-object object. Mastery exists solely in how your actions relate to what's there. There is no *thing* that is skill. It is only through re-creating your relationship to what's occurring from the ground up that you create mastery.

Relationship Cannot "Not Work." A Relationship Is Only What Is Occurring between Two or More.

A relationship is perceived when we relate one thing or person to another thing or person. When speaking about people, a relationship is determined by the actions of two or more as they relate to each other. It cannot be wrong, nor can it not work. It is working exactly as it is occurring. That is what the relationship *is*.

When it comes to people relating, whatever action someone takes, plus actions taken by another in relationship to the first action, combine to create an inter-action. An interaction does not lie outside of the very actions you take in relation to the actions of another. Your actions are what determine and create the interaction.

When you think a relationship hasn't worked out, what you're saying is that it didn't produce the results you wanted. But that is an assessment made in relationship to your desires. The relationship is actually whatever happens. So, it can't "not" work, nor can it be right or wrong. Working or not working, winning or losing, and right or wrong are assessments made by an individual. They are applied to what's observed; they are not inherent in it. They are created yet not recognized as created.

Your job is to relate effectively to whatever is occurring, so it never serves to make the other, the other's actions, or the circumstances "wrong" in your mind. What is taking place is what is occurring—circumstance, actions, situation, and so on—and your job is to learn to relate to what is occurring effectively. Knowing this changes your sense of responsibility and possibility in the matter.

Mastery Is Not Personal, Nor Is There Any "Choice" in the Matter

Sometimes people think that mastery means they can do whatever they want because they're a master. Actually, as a master you have no choice in the matter—you are far more a slave to the demands of mastery than you are the boss of them. In any endeavor, you are bound to whatever action must be taken for it to work out. You don't have the slightest choice in this, nor can it be done "your way" or through your personal style. The "rules" and requirements that determine mastery have nothing to do with an individual. These demands are impartial. The principles that govern mastery don't care who aligns with them. Yet once you are aligned, the power of the principle is realized.

A master is absolutely enslaved by the demands that determine mastery. If you want your own style, your own individuality, if you want to "do it your way," it is best to drop the notion of being masterful. You can always pretend, after the fact, that you had some say in the matter, but during the event in which your ability is demonstrated, you have no choice about what must be done. You cannot deviate one inch, nor for one moment, from the process that will produce the result that you seek. You have no choice.

An experience of this is not at all bad. As a matter of fact, it is cherished by masters of all kinds. It is an opportunity to drop the act and demands of an ego and become one with the activity of being alive. It is a powerful and rich experience that cannot be explained, nor can it be understood by anyone who has not submitted themselves to it. There is a great freedom that lies beyond an individual's style and agenda.

Interaction Is Strictly Relative; Limitation and Possibility Co-exist

Every object and every event can only exist in relationship. Yet relationship only occurs in that objects and events exist. The import or significance of this may elude you for the moment, but upon reflection it can reveal something quite profound about the nature of reality, including the nature of interaction and relationship. Because of the relative nature of existence, no possibility can manifest without limitation.

If you understand this deeply, you understand that things do not exist independently. The existence of anything arises solely in relationship. It is always relative; otherwise, it does not exist. Consider the power that is inherent and overlooked by grasping the relationship between possibility and limitation. This is not a simplistic matter; it can only be understood with unconventional insight. I'll leave that up to you.

Discover and Eliminate All Ineffective Assumptions and Beliefs

An experience of the above assertions provides a wedge to help open up your experience of relationship and your idea of mastery. Yet reinterpreting your current worldview is most often a monumental task. It requires a transformation of the framework that holds your thinking. It demands more than challenging deep-seated convictions and assumptions; it requires eliminating them.

The foundational assumptions, beliefs, and convictions you have that generate ineffective behavior or block effective interaction must be discovered and let go. Discovery is the first step, and this can be challenging because you may not know what assumptions, beliefs, and convictions you have that limit your effectiveness. Be open to looking into taken-for-granted areas of your experience and mind, and question everything's validity—then ask yourself if they could block effectiveness in some way.

Once discovered, you can let an assumption go by realizing beyond mere belief that it is false. You will know you have let go of some belief or assumption, when your very perception, thinking, and feeling are no longer influenced by it. This is not merely suppressing a belief or assumption or adopting an affectation. Rather, those habitually ingrained assumptions will no longer be active. They will become seen as empty and silly.

Analogous to this, remember something you believed when you were a child that you no longer believe. When you look back on it, the belief may look childish. Perhaps you would be embarrassed to believe it as an adult. Your life is no longer influenced by that belief, and it is not difficult for you to perceive reality without it. From this you may see the direction in which you need to go.

It is hard for people to confront that a great deal of what they believe and assume isn't actually true and is often no more useful than erroneous childish beliefs. The assertions that I have provided so far offer a contrast to some overlooked assumptions and beliefs that govern ineffective interactions. They also establish the beginning of a more effective and powerful structure of interpretation from which to take action. Yet they will only be powerful if they are contemplated, tested, and experienced as true. And there are many more assumptions and beliefs that are personal to you that you'll have to uncover and abolish for yourself.

Before we start unpacking powerful principles for mastery, let's dive into some new possibilities for learning. Perhaps addressing how we learn, and how we could learn more effectively, will help in learning these principles and assist in our pursuit of mastery.

RETHINKING LEARNING

A New Way of Learning

When you start to look for ways to increase your effectiveness, you will search in various areas. You'll likely look into knowledge received from others. You'll also try to do what it is you want to accomplish. If you fall short, even after trying harder and not being much more successful, you'll probably start to search through the data at hand to try to figure out what will make the endeavor work out.

As this process unfolds, often something is discovered that seems to help or improve your efforts. You may observe that "this feeling," "that thinking," or action directed a bit more "this way" seems to work better, shows promise, or indicates that it might move you closer to your goal. Although this process can be quite useful, there is a hidden danger here that most people overlook. The discovery is not a problem in itself. What immediately occurs, however, is that you'll draw conclusions and make assumptions about what you observed. Herein lies the danger.

What you often don't notice is that your conclusions about the cause or meaning of what has occurred are rarely correct. You give meaning to and explain what you perceive has occurred in a way that relates it to your view of the world. You will see it within the framework of your individual beliefs and relate it to what you desire or assume to be true. This process immediately reduces and restricts the discovery to a manageable form that is consistent with what you already believe.

You can see that this tends to turn you back toward the framework of the experience that you were trying to change through such discovery. Remember that your actions, and so your ability, are determined by your experience. Therefore, this dynamic puts a limitation on its possibility for success. If you cannot change in some way what or how you perceive, then you will not change your actions.

The danger here lies in the unconscious but purposeful tendency to interpret everything observed in ways that make sense to your already established belief systems. This simply aligns with the existing framework you hold; it doesn't change it. Instead, it's better to observe without bias, stretching beyond what you want to be true or believe should be true, and looking freshly at what is actually occurring without drawing knee-jerk conclusions about it.

This touches on what I consider to be a major obstacle to learning. It is difficult to communicate this obstacle because the same problem exists in hearing it as in learning anything: you hear it within your current thinking and knowledge. Often, as you listen to someone speaking of a kind or level of experience that is new, you listen with your current beliefs, assumptions, and historical background. Of course, oftentimes what people say is simply an expression of their beliefs and not an honest communication of an experience worth relating. So, you may also have become jaded to the possibility of really "hearing" a transforming experience—or in other words, hearing something that shifts your experience of reality a little or a lot.

Not only do people tend to make unconscious assumptions and conclusions about anything observed, they also often fail to fully experience and train the very breakthrough experiences that they do have. This is another way of speaking about your responsibility. Without being fully responsible, you will achieve neither breakthrough nor mastery.

Radical experimentation and experiential inquiry serve as possible doorways to breaking through the framework by which you receive all information and experience. By radical experimentation, I mean attempting actions, thinking, and feelings that go completely against the grain of what you would consider right, possible, sane, workable, or reasonable. This means being willing to engage in areas that appear contrary to what you want or believe.

Whatever you attempt in this way may well not work, but even so, you'll get feedback that can serve you in understanding why it doesn't work and so point you in a direction that may work. Also, here you can discover something that you would never have come up with otherwise. What's more, this gives you access to a new domain of thinking or avenue of investigation that expands your relationship to the matter at hand.

Experiential inquiry is not just questioning and investigating; it is looking for an authentic experience in a matter. Whenever you experience or observe some new phenomenon, don't be so quick to believe something about it or know what it is. When you experience some new feeling-state, or seem to observe a dynamic or principle, do you know what it really is, especially in the beginning? Rarely. It's likely you simply believe what someone has told you, or what you've made up for yourself, and apply this belief to the phenomenon.

In order to move past this tendency, you must learn to admit you don't really know what something is or what it means. Then you can openly investigate it further. The truth of the matter is not what you believe nor what anyone else has ever told you. Even if they were correct, coming from direct and authentic personal experience, and telling the truth—and, in all honesty, that's rare—the belief they express is not in any way the same as the experience itself. You'll need to counter the automatic tendencies to think you know right away, and instead truly listen or observe to get what's there without conjecture.

As a practice, I often encourage people not to stop at the first conclusion regarding anything they discover about why some activity works or doesn't work. I suggest you get in the habit of drawing more than one conclusion. You will find that you can make many legitimate and viable conclusions about any observation once you've continued beyond your first assumption. It's a bit like a detective trying to imagine what really happened given the evidence. Whatever scenario he comes up with to explain things can be wrong. There is more than one scenario that could explain the case, and some may not be obvious. In doing this practice, an opening is created that is even bigger than the number and profundity of the conclusions made. If more than one legitimate conclusion can be made about something, this suggests that what is observed is itself not any of the conclusions.

If not what you conclude, then what is true? That's the point: a conclusion is a different activity from an actual experience of what's true. Experiencing the truth of a matter personally and directly doesn't require a detached intellectual conclusion about what *might* be true. Knowing this helps you to ponder any matter, pushing you to inspect your conclusions with greater rigor and so increasing the likelihood your conclusions will relate to what's true more accurately.

From such a practice, you are empowered to learn more quickly and encounter new ideas, dynamics, or phenomena that aren't restricted to past patterns. In this way, you'll create a new experience that will produce new results, the effectiveness of which remains to be seen. You're also empowered to experience "existentially" what is there, meaning without bias or assumption or personal psychology clouding the matter. Such clarity lends itself to more powerful discovery and learning.

Powerful Learning

One of the necessary activities in pursuing mastery is learning. Like thinking, we imagine that learning is just one activity and we are either good at it or not. Once again, this is just not true. There are many ways to learn, and there are methods of learning that few people access. We often fall into the assumption that we have to learn "our way," that we have one way of learning that suits us. Perhaps we learn abstractly, or through a step-by-step regimen, or intuitively, or experientially, or through body-feel, or some other way. Personally, I think it's a great limitation to restrict learning to one method. Why not use them all?

We complain that we can't, that other ways of learning are for other people and are too hard for us. Perhaps it seems that way, but then again, if you change your thinking on the matter, you may well change your ability to learn and to learn in different ways. Beyond just a variety of methods of learning, what about creating new kinds of learning, even new domains of learning?

I've talked many times about learning through grasping the teacher's experience when trying to learn some skill or new experience being shared. Often people think that they not only have to learn their way, but that they must experience whatever's being taught through the filters of their own self-experience. In other words, without thinking about it, people stand on their own experience as the arbiter of what to receive and what to reject about anything shared. This creates a severe limitation on one's ability to learn. Instead, I recommend that a more effective way to learn is to temporarily "become" the other person.

A first reaction to this suggestion can be, "but I might lose myself." This reaction better reveals the dynamic I was speaking about as self-filtering. We automatically put our self-world first as the foundation for experience—and so learning—and anything shared is received as secondary and "foreign" to be accepted or rejected. On the other hand, taking on the other's experience wholesale and without filter provides a far faster way to learn. What is it that they feel, how do they look at the world, what do they think, what reality are they looking at and experiencing? These questions show the direction I'm speaking about. If I can grasp or experience what the other person is experiencing, I can do or understand whatever it is they can do and understand. See how it works?

You really don't need to worry about losing yourself, because it doesn't work that way. This dynamic applies to learning how to do something, as well as taking in and adopting what's being shared. As an example, I was once visiting my cousin in Rhode Island. He managed a thousand acres of land on which he raised pheasants and other game birds, trained hunting dogs, and provided recreation for visitors. One such recreation was sporting clays. This is a game that consists of moving through the forest to a small deck where one stands in front of a small, football goalpost-type structure situated toward the back of the deck. Clays would fly out of the forest in various directions and at various heights, all unknown. Standing with a shotgun, my job was to shoot them all out of the sky.

As a group, we'd move through the forest from deck to deck, each deck with differing setups. The idea was to create an overall score, akin to golf, to be improved over time. One of the harder shots to make was at a clay flying directly at you just overhead. With a shotgun one needs to get the stream of shot in front of the clay. So when a clay flies at the shooter, they raise the gun quickly and attempt to get in front of it. Thus, the goalpost bar behind the shooter is to stop the barrel when it is straight up, so the shooter does not accidently swing around and shoot his friends standing behind him.

For my first try at this game, my cousin partnered me with the skeet shooting champion of Massachusetts to coach me in the art. He stood just behind my shoulder and spoke into my ear about what to do or change. Having spent time learning to shoot rifles, my relationship to the shotgun was influenced by that effort. But shotguns aren't rifles and can't be used in the same way. So, when my coach would tell me to do it this way or think that way or look in this way, immediately it felt wrong to me. But I simply asked myself, "who's the master here?" And that wasn't me, but him. Recognizing this, I did my best to do exactly what he suggested.

We had fun and I learned quite a bit and improved as we progressed. As we were walking back to the lodge across the grass, my coach said to me, "You did exactly what I asked you to do. *Nobody* does what I tell them to do!" I said, "I understand, I'm a teacher also." The point to this story is that without knowing it, almost no one actually does as instructed. Instead, they listen or see but don't hear or experience what's there because of this automatic self-filtering. It is best to eliminate that, and work to get the experience "over there," or to do what you are coached to do, even if it doesn't feel right or familiar (which is necessary since if you are learning something new, it can't be familiar). Learning will not only be faster but more accurate.

We aren't restricted to this shift to create new domains of learning. Another very powerful possibility for learning starts with developing an exceptional ability to pay attention and make distinctions. Everything that occurs arises as a distinction—perceptive-experience—and so everything learned is a matter of making new distinctions. The very act or activity itself is nothing more than the distinctions that comprise it. Being able to do or grasp anything is a matter of being able to make all the distinctions that comprise that activity.

For example, perhaps you want to become a master violinist and yet have never played a violin. How would this new dimension of learning apply? First, you'd find a master violinist and watch and listen. But how can you master the violin doing that? Consider how much you already know about the objective world. You make all kinds of distinctions about weight, size, motion, vibration, and more. When I toss a brick to you you'll "feel" many distinctions about the brick—its weight, hardness, substance, and shape—and catch it, adjusting your motions to accommodate the brick. In contrast, when I toss you a rubber ball, you would respond very differently, "feeling" the weight, hardness, substance, shape, and even aerodynamics, to grasp the speed and motion of the ball and adjust your actions to those distinctions. And you make many more distinctions than these about your objective and subjective world.

Watch the person and ask yourself: What are they doing? How do they move? What do they think? Watch and "feel" what they are experiencing as well as exactly what they are doing, and every distinction in sound, movement, pressures applied, angle of bow, speed of draw, and so on. Then do it. If you can match everything that they do, you can play the violin well. Of course, without practice and personal experience it is extremely unlikely you can make all the necessary distinctions for mastery, and it may take some time to work out the basics and advance.

Even so, imagine you can re-create their mastery by learning to see, hear, and feel every aspect of what they are doing. Then add to that practicing, comparing what you produce to that of the master, and then watching the master again with a more informed experience and grasping any distinctions you missed. Do this until you have mastery. Such an approach can cut the learning time down tremendously.

Of course, if you are attempting something no one else has ever attempted or mastered, you can't use this method. But equally powerful learning can take place, just in different ways. You'll still need to grasp all of the distinctions necessary in the field, even if you are inventing the field. You'll have to create new ways of thinking and new ways of perceiving what's in front of you. If you're breaking new ground, you'll have to create new experiences from which to do it.

Now let's turn attention to some of the central principles that make things work. When it comes to effective interaction, there are fundamental principles that we'd do well to understand and incorporate.

Chapter Six
Principles and States That Empower Mastery

I've asserted that your objective is realized by relating effectively to the forces and events that are unfolding. But how this is done can be quite involved, especially in a relationship where it is the other party's job and intent to thwart your efforts and prevent you from realizing your objective. Since part of my expertise is in the fighting arts, I can ground these points in that context. But just as many fields use the principles found in Sun Tzu's *Art of War,* you must translate these principles into forms appropriate to your field of interaction.

Most of us have a real challenge translating principles learned in one field to another field, even though they might well apply. This may be one of the reasons most people don't master anything. Another reason may be because they don't attempt to grasp pertinent principles or apply them broadly, not knowing it is possible for them to do so. Commensurate with that limiting factor, people often have a difficult time grasping the principle beyond a technique, exercise, or the examples used to teach the principle. But it is possible to do so.

You need to be able to apply any learned principles to your field and to other fields as well. Unless you experientially understand the principle itself—not just the description or method used to invite you to get it— and are able to live it, breathe it, and "be" it, mastery will remain elusive.

A COUPLE ACTIONS USEFUL FOR EFFECTIVE INTERACTION

First, I would like to propose two activities that should be taken into account in order to produce the best results most effectively.

Align to the Principles of an Effortlessly Effective Body

Correct body-awareness and use obviously increases the effectiveness of and the possibilities available within any physical activity. Let's look at this assertion using just a couple of examples, those of balance and centered unity.

Balance is a key aspect of any physical activity. If my balance isn't good, I will be clumsy in my attempted actions. In all physical interactions—and metaphorically, in nonphysical interactions—balance is essential. Without balance one loses power, mobility, responsiveness, ability, and so on. So, we can see that remaining well-balanced should be a constant.

For example, without good balance I can't immediately move in any direction that I want. If I am falling a bit to the left, for instance, I can't suddenly leap to my right. This restricts what possible actions I can take in the interaction, thus restricting the amount of actions available to me as well as my ability to do them.

Apply the principle of balance to your domain and notice that even if your field is primarily non-objective, this principle still contributes to your effectiveness. In business, for example, you can see that being balanced in your own mind, in your relationships with others, and in your plans and actions will always increase effectiveness. If your strategy is not balanced, perhaps leaning blindly in one direction and leaving yourself exposed in another, you can be devastated by incorrect assessments or unexpected developments. On the other hand, if you are balanced in your dealings and strategy, when the unexpected occurs you are better able to manage it and make appropriate changes.

Balance is only one principle. This same dynamic applies to every other body principle, such as always being sensitive and aware of the whole body, being centered, being relaxed, being calm, aligning to the proper structural elements of the body, and so on. Being sensitive to and aware of the body and keeping it constantly aligned to the principles that are most effective and effortless allows the greatest chance for being skillful.

As I've mentioned, a fundamental shift that assists greatly in unifying all of the needed, refined distinctions into one effective experience is translating each of these distinctions into one feeling-sense. When it comes to physical actions, a powerful commensurate feeling-sense is to position your feeling-attention in the center region of the body, and connect the whole body to the center. This helps unify and relate all that is occurring in every part of the body into one balanced feeling-experience. It provides a body awareness and orientation that accomplishes in one instant what might otherwise require many longer or abstract processes to accomplish.

This central feeling-awareness allows you to receive incoming data in a form that is appropriate to a creative response. In physical endeavors, it relates to and unifies all parts of the body so they can work together more efficiently. It allows a sense of relationship to everything that is going on as a whole with others and your own body in each moment. In social or business or dialogue-based interactions, feeling-awareness also serves to ground your experience and keep it from becoming overly intellectual or abstract, and it brings about a stronger sense of presence and certainty.

Decades ago I used to teach a body-being course that was open to anyone. One course was attended by the then University of California Berkeley water polo team captain. In the next course, he came back and brought the entire team. Of course, the principles and dynamics taught had to be applied to being in water and the actions of water polo, but after the course that year they won the U.S. water polo championships. Did the body-being work contribute to their success? I like to think so.

Although these principles are essential for mastery in a physical endeavor, they are also quite useful in the nonphysical domains. Have you ever noticed that someone's posture and body presence influences not only how they are received, but also indicates what they think of themselves and their level or lack of confidence? When someone exudes a sense of being centered, or has an air of spatial awareness, this will be seen as powerful and solid and influence the assessment of others. One's physical awareness has an impact on nonphysical aspects of relationship, and as mentioned, the various principles involved can be applied powerfully in an appropriate form to your particular endeavor.

Being balanced or centered are just two principles. I use them as examples, but remember, you must always leap beyond the examples. What other principles are there? Think about it. How is a body designed? What forces are constantly acting on the body? What influence do mind, awareness, and perspective have on physical performance? Of course, I've invited you to read *Zen Body-Being* to delve more deeply into these principles, but you also have to do your own homework. Consider the matter, investigate, study, and look into the overlooked obvious.

～

Keep an effortlessly effective and sensitive
body awareness.

～

Practice Creating Alternative Strategies

It is good to open your mind to the fact that there's more than one avenue to accomplishing a goal. Given your objective and immediate goals, and the practicality of attaining those goals, you can always recognize a number of possible paths to produce a desired result. It is a valuable practice to ascertain as many possible paths as you can at every stage of the interaction.

When I was learning to play Go—a Chinese board game with black and white stones on a 19×19 grid, the possible patterns of which are astoundingly large—I would try to figure out my next move. When I'd consider putting a stone down in one place, it would mean that my opponent could make any number of moves relating to it. Unlike chess, he can place his stone anywhere on the board. But I noticed that when I tried to extrapolate out possible outcomes, my brain would shut down at about five possibilities. My thinking would go something like this: "If I put my stone here, he might put his stone there, and if that happens then I could put my next stone there, and then he might put a stone over here, so then I could put a stone there, and he might . . . " And then my brain would shut down.

So, I'd try again. And again. At any point he could put a stone in several different places, and so I'd have to follow each probability out. The possibilities were multiple, even when restricted to the immediate area of play. I found that over time, as I forced my brain not to shut down but to stay with it, I became more skilled. After a good deal of work, I could follow out many permutations much more quickly. Eventually, this became knowing many possibilities at a glance without having to go through a step-by-step accounting. This same basic lesson applies to every other field as well. Concentrate on working out different possibilities that could unfold, and create various plans to meet them. Practice over and over until this ability slips into more of an automatic perception of every probable possibility all at once.

In each moment, your awareness must include you and any objects or others involved, whatever is occurring, and the possibilities for appropriate actions that appear within all this. If at any moment your activity is not working out well, you should be able to seamlessly change, switching to another path—to one of the other possibilities you've already gleaned. Of course, it takes practice to develop the ability to discern when change is needed and what direction it should take. Sometimes it will be obvious that what you're doing isn't working, or you can tell that continuing to follow your current strategy will not produce the result you want. At these times, you need to change—immediately.

When you become adept at recognizing various paths and strategies in each moment, such change is made more easily accessible. As you receive feedback during the unfolding interaction, you may recognize that one of your other paths would be far more appropriate given what's happening, or you may realize that you need to come up with a totally new set of paths and strategies. With practice, this awareness will tend to occur naturally; it will become commonplace and simply a new and sophisticated aspect of your perception and interpretation.

People sometimes think that masters simply do an action and it turns out well because those people are good at that action. The truth is most often, and especially within interactions, that the master is making subtle adjustments throughout the process from beginning to end. Within the projected possibilities, the most effortless path should be sought out. Ask: Which of the paths would be most effortless as well as effective? This helps discern more subtle but important factors. It also assists in choosing the most appropriate course of action at the time.

Follow a plan of action only as long as it continues to fit the circumstances. The moment the slightest change occurs that warrants it, immediately shift the process in a new direction or to a new plan. This allows your extrapolations to be extremely plastic, arising newly in every moment.

~

Never jump to conclusions;
wait for them.

~

A FEW ESSENTIAL PRINCIPLES

In addition to the actions described above, I would like to offer a few principles that assist in making interaction more effective.

Don't Ignore

The first principle is the inclusion of factors not attended. There is always something that you're ignoring or, for some reason, of which you are not aware. By being aware of and sensitive to this condition you can constantly turn your attention to what's not being attended.

This itself does not remedy the problem. But it does allow you to be presently aware of it in your experience and thus take it into account while being open to discovering something not previously noticed. This empowers you to notice anything you have missed, suppressed, or ignored, and helps you recognize information that was overlooked.

The Effortless Principle

As previously mentioned, another element that can be very empowering, helping to increase discovery and achieve mastery, is the principle of effortlessness. You can accomplish your goals in various ways. Depending on what you're dealing with, sometimes you will do this with stress and strain, brute force, or coercion, or there may be a lot of work or effort put into your attempt, but the end goal should be to learn to achieve results effortlessly. The principle of searching for the most effortless approach forces you to look in directions you otherwise wouldn't have sought out.

The use of effort is a natural response when trying to get something done. It may be an automatic tendency, but it isn't necessarily the best approach. People value, and so will often focus on, getting the result no matter how they get it, rather than studying the processes or principles that lead to the result. Therefore, the very idea of finding the process that provides the most effortlessly attained results doesn't occur to them as something to pursue.

Simply asking the question "how can the result be achieved effortlessly?" opens up new possibilities for mastery. In order to pursue mastery, you need to search out the most effective ways to do things, and the best answer almost always corresponds to the most effortless way. This is true because doing something effortlessly requires greater precision and a deeper understanding of and alignment to the principles and dynamics that can make it that way. And mastery demands the same level of precision and alignment.

Adopting this principle forces you to confront unconventional ideas and reimagine what's possible. It forces you to inspect more thoroughly how things really work and how they could work. You must take apart the elements that comprise your endeavor and push past your assumptions to discover what is really there. You are also forced to stop overlooking the obvious and develop a much deeper understanding of the existential nature of your field of mastery. Effortlessness requires making many more refined distinctions, and this experience empowers mastering your endeavor.

When you look at anyone whom you consider a master of their craft or art, the chances are high that they look effortless doing it. Why is that? Perhaps because there is a connection between effortlessness and mastery. If you ski, you might remember, in the beginning, putting a great deal of effort into managing to stay upright. But when you got good at it, you simply swooshed smoothly and easily down the slopes. Learning to ride and jump horses seems to require padding inside the knees and soreness afterward, but when you're good at it you can do it without padding and don't need ice when you're done. If you look at football teams you see those that use brute strength and size to accomplish their goals, and then you see those that are more like dancers, using mobility and grace and skill to win. Although the more effortless team doesn't always win, they are always more skillful, because they have to be. I'm sure you can come up with many other examples. Instead of achieving effortlessness after mastering something, use the effortless principle to help you master it.

Mind-Body Alignment Principle

I already touched briefly on this very important principle. The mind-body alignment principle improves your levels of effectiveness and power a great deal. In physical endeavors of any kind this principle will improve one's ability to accomplish any result, as well as the ease and power with which it can be done. This principle applies to any action or interaction, whether physical or not. Thinking, communicating, socializing, building, and so on can all be improved by understanding and aligning to this principle. Any process undertaken is improved greatly with the mind-body alignment principle in operation.

The first aspect of the principle is to understand a dynamic that you may engage in (since pretty much everyone does)—that weakens your power and effectiveness. This is separating the activity of your mind from the activity of the process you are in. For example, if you want to move an object from one place to another, you will grab the object and immediately start thinking about the place you want the object to go. When that happens, your body, mostly your head, will begin to orient to the place where you imagine the outcome, and you will likely turn to look at the space where the end result is expected. This is because your mind moves much faster than any physical process in which you engage. You can conceptualize being across the room, for example, much more quickly than you can walk or even run there.

In any case, when the mind moves ahead of the process as it's unfolding, a split will happen and you will find yourself relating to a future projection, rather than to the occurring process in each moment. This weakens the process a great deal. It also tends to lead to frustration as you try to bridge the gap between the mind's desire and the activity, often by using force. Instead, when you keep the mind riveted and focused solely on the process in real time, you are not split and you gain tremendous power. In every miniscule segment of the process or action, the mind should be fused with and doing only that throughout the process—neither falling behind nor jumping ahead.

When confronted with this assertion, some people say: "What if I forget where I'm going?" or "Don't I need to focus on the result in order to get there?" This principle does seem to fly in the face of such taken for granted "wisdom" of focusing on the result. Yet such result-oriented focus is not the best approach.

There is no way you will forget the result, even if you don't give it any thought whatsoever. The reason you're engaged in the process or the activity at all *is* to produce the result. The result is inherent in the process itself. As a matter of fact, the result is simply the part of the process you're doing the process for. So, you don't have to give it a second thought; the moment you enter the process, the result is already present.

This principle demands you keep your attention and focus completely on the process each step of the way. Melding mind and action together increases the power and effectiveness of the action. Try it. But remember, it takes "mind control," so stay alert to the automatic tendencies of mind to leap ahead, get distracted, or introduce elements not relevant, which may be overlooked.

In any physical activity, aligning the entire body to the task at hand is an essential part of this principle. The overwhelming tendency for people is to have many parts of the body, grossly and subtly, moving in wrong directions as they relate to the thought of the desired result. But in doing so these parts are not truly aligned to the task. This takes a lot of careful study to correct.

As an example, if you were to push your hand into a heavy object with a bent arm, like in a hook punch, your face is likely to turn toward the direction you want the object to go. Your shoulder may well lean in that direction as well, as will your hips, and so on. This will cause strain, especially in your shoulder, and will weaken your efforts—most of your body will not be moving into the hand, even though you may think it is.

On the other hand, it is much more powerful to keep your gaze on the process as it unfolds, and not move ahead of it, with your shoulder behind and moving around toward the elbow, and then the elbow into the hand, and then the hips backing up the shoulder, and so on, so that every part of the body is aligned perfectly to the task and not moving in any other direction. This is not to say that every body part moves grossly in the same direction, but that each part is moving in the exact direction that it needs to be going in order to support every other part and align to the task.

Recall the room full of marbles mental exercise when you imagined tracing paths from one marble to the next in all sorts of geometric patterns. Now, imagine each marble moving directly into the one next to it in a complex pattern so that every marble is moving exactly in the direction it should to support the end marble of the pattern. In a spiral, for example, some marbles will be moving in the opposite direction from others in the same moment—in fact, many marbles will be moving in different directions—but they should all be moving to support the spiral.

Compare this to billiards. In this game, one ball may go in one direction to move another ball in a very different direction, but in the end, if both move in the exact direction they should, the end ball goes where it should.

If all your millions of body parts are aligned, each moving in the exact direction it should—without any strain or forcing or binding any one part to any other—they will all serve the task perfectly. This is how every part of your entire body—or in other fields, all parts of any given process, objective or not—should be aligned in its service to the task. Doing this reduces the amount of strain to zero, lessens the needed effort a great deal, and increases the power and effectiveness as well as the efficiency of any action or process.

In non-objective endeavors, all of the activities that contribute to a process should directly support the objective. With care, you will likely find aspects that are not really serving, or are moving in directions that are off purpose, or are even counterproductive. Bringing all the disparate parts into alignment for each segment of a process increases their power multifold. The mind-body alignment principle is a very valuable asset for increasing power and effectiveness and reducing strain.

The Power of Correction

Correction and creative intelligence are both necessary ingredients for mastery. Most people probably wouldn't connect correction with mastery. But then again, most people don't experience mastery. The correction that I am speaking of is not only a necessary component for *attaining* mastery but is also necessary for *being* masterful.

Intelligence, on the other hand, is a more graciously received component. You likely suspect that some form of intelligence might be required in order to master something. Yet again, the intelligence of which I speak eludes most of us as an active and fully functioning ingredient. I will try to provide a springboard from which to make the leap in experience and understanding necessary to grasp what I am referring to as these two principles of mastery.

Correction is changing whatever is not effective into what is. It is shifting the course of action from what does not work, or is not working, to what does. This shift can require a change in thinking, perception, interpretation, impulse, movement, attitude, emotion, or any other component that makes up the activity you're doing. You will need to isolate the factors involved that need to change. It could be many or a few.

For example, if we are playing catch, and I throw the ball toward the door, but you are standing by the window, I might wonder why you don't catch the ball. After some consideration, I isolate direction as a factor. Now I can make a correction in the direction I throw the ball. Of course, I may be assuming that balls must be tossed toward doors, or I may have some emotional resistance to aiming at windows, or there may be any number of subjective or physical components that keep me from being effective that also need to change in order to successfully change my actions.

As you take an action, you will receive feedback about the effectiveness of your action. The more you know about what is necessary to realize an objective—the more sensitive you are to *what* must occur and *when* it must occur—the sooner you will know, and with greater accuracy, whether the process is going to work out or not. If you ascertain that it is not going to work out via your present course of action, you must change your actions.

This holds true for any kind of interaction. If, in the course of a conversation, for example, you recognize that the objective of the dialogue is not being realized, you must change your communication. Perhaps the objective for the conversation is to solve a problem, and the speaking has slipped into a sidetrack that will not get the problem solved. Then the conversation must be redirected back on track with the intent to come up with a solution to this problem.

Once, I was playing a game of Go with a high-ranking player. Since I was pretty much self-taught, and a relative novice, I didn't expect to win, even though I had won every game I played up to that point. I was correct in my assessment; he did moves I'd never seen before and finally ended up beating me. I asked for another game, which was granted. This time I actually beat him, and as we put away the stones he made this comment: "You didn't play at all like you did the first time." I replied, "Of course not. I lost the first time." Fast learning and correction, and adopting new strategies, actions, and even thinking, are necessary when needed.

Layers

Correction needs to occur within many different timeframes. You must make corrections in the shortest period of time as well as in relation to accomplishing a long-term objective or building something that may take years. There are many layers and cycles involved in most processes.

All of them have to be taken into account, and your actions must relate to them all.

Suppose that in a game, such as a boxing match, the feedback suggests that you are losing. You're getting hit more frequently than the opponent, you don't seem to be able to control the fight, and you are awkward, frustrated, and dazed. This clearly suggests that what you are doing is not working to win this fight. You must change your actions. Probably you also need to change your thinking, attitude, and definitely your strategy and movements.

However, these changes cannot be random—they must improve your effectiveness. Of course, since you are losing, any change stands a better chance of winning than what you're doing. Yet you would like to change in a way that helps you win. This requires some understanding regarding why you are losing and what has to take place to win given these circumstances and this opponent. If this is understood correctly, then you have established a direction in which to proceed. Your actions can now be designed to accomplish this shift. I call this fast problem-solving.

When Muhammad Ali fought George Foreman, we could see a change in strategy unfold. His first round he danced and boxed, testing George and feeling his power. Realizing this strategy wasn't going to work, he changed to his newly invented strategy called "rope-a-dope," angering Foreman on purpose and then letting him tire himself by pounding Ali as Ali rode on the ropes. In the end, the strategy worked, and Ali was able to knock out an exhausted Foreman.

In a boxing example, you can see how you must not only be concerned with the big picture, you must also be concerned with every instant. As you proceed with any process, such as throwing a punch, you obtain feedback as to the status of your action relative to the process you are trying to accomplish. Are you in the right position to begin? Are the opponent's structure and movement forming up as you predicted at the right stage of the process? Does he recognize yet what is happening? How do you proceed if he does? Is the angle of your force correct? Have you perceived the opponent's force and actions completely? These are all questions that need attention in a very short segment of time. As you proceed, if any of the requirements for an effective process are not being met, you must change the course of your actions so that they are.

In some highly demanding fields, like fighting, this can and must be done in every millisecond. You need to know where your opponent is and what they are doing. So you will engage in the process of looking at them to perceive what is happening. This is a very short process; yet without having successfully directed it toward the purpose at hand, you would be unable to proceed with the rest of the interaction effectively.

If all of the immediate processes occur in relation to your objective, and undergo correction so that they remain on track, then you can build a larger process made up of the smaller ones. This may require moving through many different attempted actions, combining them successfully, using the beginning of one and the middle of another, setting up a combination of actions designed to create an opening for still another action, or even creating new activities on the spot. You may need to change your strategy, your tactics, and probably your spirit and sensitivity throughout the whole endeavor. All these changes should be made until the larger process leads to your desired result. You must therefore be in a position of making constant correction in every moment.

An uncle—who engaged very successfully in international business—once told me: "Most people take on a strategy and stick to it regardless of changes in conditions. This is a big mistake. For example, when new international laws are passed, they affect everyone. The people that are successful are the ones who learn to cope and change sooner rather than later." I found this consistent with my own experience of success.

Extrapolation

Things often don't turn out exactly as you plan or expect they will. As was seen in the non-objective distinction of extrapolation, you will commit to a course of action based on what you have perceived up to the moment of action. This will take into account what has occurred over time, such as how someone has acted in the past, and what has just occurred in recent moments. Whatever you think to do will be determined by your experience of history—recent history and lifetime history—but your actions will be directed toward the future.

The future, however, does not exist. Therefore, the strategy, the plan, and the extrapolated assessment arise as ideas, thoughts, and images. Whatever form they take, it's always conceptual. This means that it is not, and cannot be, a reflection of what is going to happen, because it has not happened yet. So it must be subject to correction. Which is to say, even if the extrapolation and plan are superbly done, and are indeed an exact fit for what is expected to happen, they will not and cannot be what actually happens. They are a best guess and an image, or mock conceptual experience, of what will happen, and this will be different from the real thing. An experience of something is different from the concept of something.

Perception vs. Concept

One thing you can do to ameliorate this condition is to train your conceptualizing to replicate your experience exactly. Many people are very sloppy when it comes to conceiving things and events. They remember something, but it is often inaccurate and not as it was perceived, and they don't notice this discrepancy. Without noticing and studying it, you can't improve on it. Any decisions you make with a sloppy concept will relate to the errors or missing elements of your reproduction, and not to the actual thing or event, and so you will make mistakes and be ineffective in relation to that thing or event. Try the next exercise to get a handle on this dynamic and start improving your ability to create accurate representations.

■   Concept vs. Perception Exercise   ■

Take a moment to look up at a stationary scene that is occurring near you, such as the wall in front of you or whatever stationary objects are within view. Once you've gazed at it for a moment, close your eyes and try to reproduce the scene exactly as it is. This isn't about memorizing; just try to see in your mind's eye what you saw when your eyes were open.

After you've done the best you can, open your eyes and look again. Notice that what you see is different from what you imagined, and notice exactly how it is different (distance, size, dimension, colors, proportions, and so on). Then close your eyes again and repeat. Remember, this is not about memorizing, it is about looking; simply look briefly to see what's there, and then close your eyes.

When ready, open and check, and do it all again. As you do, increase your ability to reproduce the scene exactly. Even include in your conceptual image the distinctions of "real" and "present" and "there" and "solid," and whatever else exists when you are actually perceiving the scene. Try to get to a place where you can hardly tell if your eyes are open or closed.

With this practice, you learn not only that your conceptual reproductions have been flawed, but also how to begin training your mind to reproduce things more accurately. Work to apply this to other scenes, but also to what someone said, what happened during an interaction, and so on. Work to reproduce things accurately.

It is best if you can find ways to receive feedback after the fact, such as recording a conversation and, later, after reproducing it in your mind, comparing what you recall to the recording (but trying to hear it exactly as is). Or you can revisit some place you've been after detailing it in your mind, and see if you got it right. With practice, you'll begin to improve as well as notice where you usually slip up, so you can better catch yourself in the act and make corrections before you fix things up in your mind. When you can more closely match conceptually reproducing what's there with your perceptive-experience of what's there, you will be more effective at extrapolation and making plans. No matter how good you get, however, the plan will not be the same as what occurs.

Remember a time when you planned something, like a party, or just a trip to the store. No matter how good your planning was, and how much the event seemed to turn out exactly as planned, the event-happening was a different experience than the event-planned, wasn't it? You may take this so much for granted that you have trouble at first getting what I am saying. I'm saying that concept and experience exist in different domains; they are not the same thing. Have you ever thought of being with your lover, imagined what it would be like when you met? Now, wasn't the experience of being with your lover, no matter how closely it followed your imagination, different than the concept? If not, have I got a bridge to sell you!

What is frequently the case is that the event clearly does not match the plan. The guests don't arrive on time for the party, you get sick from the dip, or you get to the store and they're out of soap. You didn't plan for these things. What you'll do, of course, is begin to tailor your plan to the circumstances or drop it and create a new plan. Frequently, you'll do this without much attention, especially if the circumstance seems to closely match your plan. If it doesn't match at all, you may get irritated or simply admit it didn't work out.

In a more immediately demanding set of circumstances, like fast-moving interactive endeavors, your relation to ever-changing circumstances must be more fluid. Therefore, constant correction is a must. It is what being skillful is all about. Usually people assume that someone who is skillful at something doesn't make any mistakes and proceeds through the event simply "doing the right thing." This is rarely true.

People who are skillful not only know what they're doing, they know what they should not do as well. They are acutely aware of what is not effective in their own actions. The reason they are skillful is because they correct their actions whenever the actions begin to be inappropriate. If this is done fluidly and quickly, it appears to others that the skillful person is simply doing well. It may even appear to the skillful person as if he or she is simply doing the right thing. But I'm asserting that skill is impossible without constant effective, even if subtle, correction, and the best time to do that is before it is needed. This is the power that keeps the action on purpose and appropriate to the ever-changing circumstances. Correction is not "bad." It's a power.

Not Falling Behind

From this observation, it seems that the best we can do is to be just a fraction behind the occurring event. If you plan something, and in the next instant circumstances change, you must redesign your plan on the spot. This is always the case, and so you will always be "behind" the arising event, either by a little or a lot. Since you want to transform your experience to become a "reflection" of the occurring event, the closer in time your experience and strategy are to what is happening, the more closely your actions will match and relate to what is happening.

If I move my body, and you see it moving, you can then try to move your own body in a way that relates to my movement. Still, however, your action will occur a little later than my movement, since you have to first see it, recognize a pattern, and create an extrapolation in order to follow it. This can all go on at an incredible speed, and the faster you can do it, the better, but you will nonetheless be trailing behind. This would not be so bad, except that I can change my actions, and you may be stuck in an extrapolation that no longer relates to my occurring movement. As I change, you must recognize the change as soon as possible so that you can create a new extrapolation, plan, and action. This is correction.

If your actions are always behind another's actions, how can you ever truly match their actions and take control? You could take action in front of an extrapolation—that is, by acting in relation to what you think is going to happen, rather than what is happening. This would be like shooting at a duck by shooting in front of its path, so that when the buckshot reaches the space in front of the duck, the duck will fly into the buckshot. Of course, this depends on the duck continuing to fly in the same direction. If the duck turned in another direction, you would miss. So it is with your actions. Although a certain amount of moving in relation to the extrapolation is appropriate, you must always bear in mind that changes are to be expected and not depend on jumping ahead as a solution to this problem.

So, what is a solution? If another is involved, the more accurately you can read and remain in touch with the other's intent, the more accurately you can design your action to occur *with* their actions and not behind them. Action follows intent. When the intent changes, so does the action. If you follow the other's intent, you are in a position to match any action that arises from this intent. In this way, you can be in relationship with the occurring event and can take control of the interaction.

As I have said elsewhere:

> *Watch the water, not the fish.*
>
> • • •
>
> *See the road they are on*
> *and you will know which way*
> *they must turn.*

If you see that to which the other is bound, you will know what actions they will take.

Having a reflective experience of another's intent is much more immediate than recognizing patterns in movement or process. You can pick up intent all at once, so to speak. Doing so tells you a great deal about any action the other(s) will take. It reveals their strategy and extrapolation and thus presents the course of action that will be taken and the impulse they'll choose to motivate this action. You can create a relationship where their intent also sparks your actions at the same time it does theirs.

A masterful samurai was once asked a question about why he was so good at winning, and his response was: *"I don't know anything about winning, I simply know how not to fall behind."*

Transforming Reaction into Response

Correction can become infinitesimally small. Earlier we addressed the difference between reaction and response. As we've seen, our general automatic tendency with input that is challenging is to react instead of responding appropriately, especially when the input is sudden or unexpected. But it is better to create an appropriate response than to succumb to a mindless reaction. An example of this is transforming a flinch into an evasion.

It rarely occurs to people that this level of transformation is possible. For example, when you perceive some object moving rapidly toward your head only a fraction of a second before impact, the general reaction is to flinch—to wince, screw up the face, turn the head a bit, tense up, and prepare for impact. This all occurs in a fraction of a second. Generally, you will be of the disposition that you are caught in a bad situation with no way out, and the best you can do is wait it out. However, if you have enough energy to flinch, why not evade? The flinch is like a paralysis, yet a great deal of energy is devoted to making it happen.

So what if you could somehow transform the very energy devoted to a reaction into a response, such as dodging the blow instead of devoting that same energy to flinching? It takes some doing, yet it is possible. It requires pushing your consciousness into the very place from which reaction arises. In that place, demand that the impulse be one of taking action, like a response, rather than a flinch. You can actually manage to dodge punches even when they are seemingly a millisecond from impact, rather than flinching.

This kind of study is fascinating work. It moves you into a domain that counters a great many of the habits and tendencies that are entrenched in overlooked assumptions about what's possible or not, and what you can and can't do. Now, apply this same depth of consideration to your field of interaction. What do you assume is inevitable but doesn't work? See what actions or reactions, states of mind or emotions would be useful to transform—even if you assume it's impossible—and consider how it can be done.

The principle of correction must also be applied to the framework in which you perceive things, including yourself. Whenever you consider what you can and can't do, and restrict your possibilities to the idea that the reality of you must be *that* way, your view of your abilities is already fixed. You have frozen your relationship to the building blocks on which you, as a person, are founded. There is little possibility for creativity in that position.

On the other hand, you can change or correct the very notions that you hold as necessary or true, if they are neither necessary nor true. To do that, you need to create an opening through which you can step away from the underpinnings of your convictions about the way you are and how it all works. This is usually a monumental undertaking. Yet such undertakings make mastery possible.

Elements of Correction
Not Knowing

One of the most important and powerful aspects for creating intelligent correction is not-knowing. In our desperate rush to know things, to be right, to not look the fool—and to figure out what to do, how to do it, and have all the answers—we tend to suppress the presence of not-knowing. Instead of realizing the power and grace not-knowing provides, we are busy trying to ignore it, avoid it, and deny it. We don't like not knowing and we certainly don't want to be wrong.

The problem with this is that not-knowing is a fact—you have no choice in the matter. Not-knowing is a constant aspect of your experience, even as you also know things. The good news is that it is not something to be avoided, but is a fundamental, inherent, and necessary aspect of being alive and learning. Learning and discovery can't occur unless you first don't know something. Therefore, mastery can't really be pursued without it. Although you can become conscious of much of what you don't know, there is a significant role for not-knowing.

Not-knowing provides an open or empty slate from which to recognize overlooked assumptions. It provides the opening necessary to challenge any conclusion, as well as the opportunity to stay in relationship to events as they arise and change. It short-circuits the overwhelming tendency to be attached to an extrapolation and allows your actions to more readily be free of historical patterns. This is all necessary if you are going to stay current and constantly open to change.

How is it possible to commit to action and yet not know? Both knowing and not-knowing need to be active. If you have to choose between the two, or are indecisive about acting because something is not known, you will lose your effectiveness. If, however, you simply admit the truth—that you indeed don't know everything that is going to happen, though you have made the most viable and honest interpretation that you can—you don't have to deny anything.

You are at once committed to the strongest course of action that appears to you and at the same time open to learning or perceiving new information and changing your actions and strategy if needed. Your commitment is to what is effective, not to a plan. With such a disposition, you can make correction without resistance. This power or ability is only possible when your feeling-awareness is allowed to bask in the presence of not-knowing as a foundational element for your analysis of what *is* known.

Freedom from Assumptions

Another element needed for correction is the recognition of ineffective assumptions. When you stand on an assumption as if it is the truth, then the only course of action lies in somehow dealing with what, perhaps in error, seems to be simply so. You need to be able to recognize when you assume something that gets in the way of being effective, and change it. This doesn't guarantee anything, but it does create an opening for correction.

Once again, let me use an example from the fighting domain that can be applied to other domains. Suppose I am playing with someone, and every time I attempt a technique he thwarts my actions. Because I assume his actions resist me in order to make me look bad, I begin to get upset. With this attitude, I am struggling with him and can only succeed if I can beat his resistance. So, without noticing it, I have put myself in resistance to his resistance.

From this assumption and my disposition, I see few possibilities available to me. Perhaps I try to trick him somehow so that I can be successful. Maybe I use more force to try to break down his resistance—and this would likely be done in anger. I might try to be faster than him and manage to slip in some move before he can react. Yet as I attempt any of these, I continue to struggle and fail.

On the other hand, by recognizing and dropping my ineffective perspective, I can see that he is merely doing his job as best he can. If he did not, I would have no one to play with. He is not trying to make me look bad; he is trying to be successful. These are different.

When I realize he is only doing his job, and that it is not personal, I suddenly cease to be in resistance to his actions or reactions. The possibility opens up that I can allow him to do what he is doing and take action accordingly. This perspective allows me to *include* his actions, changing my actions to *join* with his resistance and take over the activity, directing it toward a different outcome. This is a form of correction. But I couldn't do it without first dropping my assumption.

You must be able to see when you are stuck in assumptions or in a perspective that's not working. Once an assumption is recognized, two more elements are needed for correction: letting go and generating. Dropping the assumption, you'll also need to let go of what you are doing, thinking, and so on—which are founded on the assumption, and so are ineffective—and then generate something new, and perhaps unfamiliar to you, that works.

Creative Intelligence

We have explored many of the dynamics required to be effective in both nonphysical and physical interactions. Given the set of circumstances that make up any particular interaction, you are still left with the responsibility and task of choosing the very activity that will be effortlessly effective. Choosing an appropriate experience and action is dependent on one last factor—creative intelligence. However you accomplish it—through study and consideration, experience and wisdom, questioning and investigating, contemplation and insight—some form of intelligence is a must.

Intelligence is the final ingredient when all the other ingredients have been accounted for. It is what makes everything work. This intelligence is one of insight. Real intelligence always appears as whole and inclusive. Your awareness, attention, and state of mind should be positioned to include everything that is arising. Nothing should be shut out or overlooked. True intelligence is free from predetermined design. It may create design, but it has no attachment to any design and is not predesigned itself. It operates outside of fear and ambition and without attachment to winning or losing.

This intelligence does not assume what you interpret is a fixed reality but questions everything as possibly an assumption. It does not overlook the obvious. It also includes an ability to hold various possible interpretations and to move freely through these possibilities or create new ones spontaneously. In this way, your experience becomes plastic and less binding, allowing for a greater fluidity in making changes and an increased creativity in problem solving. With such intelligence, you view yourself as responsible for your perspective and actions. As such, you are positioned at the source of whatever you experience.

Adding a contemplative component creates the possibility of getting to the bottom of anything suppressed, unclear, or unknown in your experience. Furthermore, this intelligence cannot truly function without an overwhelming sense of honesty. Whatever is fundamentally true for you, on any level, must be acknowledged. The heart of creative intelligence is an honesty beyond the norm. Such honesty is necessary because mastery can't be founded on anything except what is really occurring and how it really occurs. If you unknowingly or knowingly distort or ignore or lie about what's true in yourself or others or the situation, you can't see clearly or relate to what's occurring, and so you won't be genuinely effective.

Such insightful intelligence works on many levels at once, bringing every relevant aspect together, making the conglomerate experience highly sophisticated and thoroughly tailored to each particular circumstance. This requires a lot of experiential knowing. Conversely, the strength of this intelligence is founded on the presence and power of a genuine not-knowing. Both are needed. Through practice you create a new experience that is informed by past learning, and at the same time you remain current and open by activating not-knowing, thus creating an uncommon wisdom in your field.

One thing I have noticed over time, in my field, is that I have the ability to change where most do not, to study how things are going and create new strategies and actions and invent new relationships as I go. For me this is just fast problem-solving, but I have noticed that most people don't access this kind of creative intelligence. It seems such an unnecessary limitation, and yet they don't seem to grasp that much more than what they have is available and instead stick to their fixed programs and simplistic perspective. But whole domains or principles can be created that change one's perspective and actions and so transform the relationship from one that isn't working well to one that is. It seems ill-advised not to take advantage of this possibility.

How do you make a shift to access such a new ability? It is both simple and complex. You "sense" or intuit the most viable and appropriate experiential state to adopt that is best suited to realize your objectives, given the circumstances of the moment. Of course, this takes some creativity, because you may have to come up with unusual possibilities. Once you discern this state, immediately adopt it. At first this is done regardless of and without concern for the practical attainability of your goals. From this state, the "how" of it becomes obvious as you relate your objectives to what's there. In doing so, what appears as an obstacle is isolated over and against the field of possibility. It is either transformed immediately, or "fast problem-solving" is undertaken.

The Need to Internalize

These principles are a lot to take in. Hearing them is only the first step on a long journey. Each distinction and principle needs to be investigated, contemplated, and absorbed, then put into action. Practicing them, finding errors in understanding, making corrections, and then practicing them even more, are all necessary for progress. Take each principle and work it until it is an accessible part of your experience. Once this is accomplished, you need to put them together into groups, creating an overall experience that includes several principles working together to form a new and more sophisticated experience. Finally, when all these elements come together into one experience, you will attain mastery.

Unfortunately, you won't be able to be effective with all this when it remains mere hearsay or intellectual abstraction. The actions you take must be based on an experience that has already internalized all of these disparate parts into one powerful awareness that "knows" what to do in each moment. Granted, there may well be times when you need to revisit or remind yourself of these points, even after you've mastered some domain of interaction or endeavor, especially since there is so much to absorb. You may well adopt a principle that works and yet, being human, your mind may slip into another focus, forgetting the principle or letting it slip away. At such a moment, you have to grasp that this has happened and re-adopt the principle—perhaps creating sort of a refresher course to get back on track. But eventually the experience of all this needs to become part of your perception and relating. It should become simply your normal experience of your field—and yourself within it.

In short, I once saw a cartoon in which two professors were standing next to a gigantic blackboard. On the blackboard was an incredibly long and complex equation stretching across and down to the bottom of the board. At the end of the equation was written "and then a miracle happens." I feel like I have given you the equation and left you with: "and now make a miracle happen."

Chapter Seven
Powerful Operating Principles for Mastery

As you can see so far, the task of making a fundamental and demonstrative shift in your abilities will likely be immense. It requires plunging into the heart of your own nature, and creating a functional context from which mastery can emerge. So, again, how can you bring all of the components of effective interaction together? You must find the principles that do just that. It might be useful to look again at the nature of a principle in the earlier section "Practice, Principle, Being" (p. 35).

The work we've gone over so far lays the necessary foundation to really make use of upcoming governing principles that will help you to become masterful. Without doing the previous work, your foundation will be weak and any attempt at adopting the principles I'm about to share will be far less effective. Even though they will improve your skill level, if you do not have a solid foundation, you won't attain mastery.

I once was teaching a professional boxer who came to me and wanted private lessons every day. He was a heavyweight. One of the first things I did was get him to drop his assumptions about being a heavyweight and got him to move more like a lightweight. Then, I spent months teaching him the material in *Zen Body-Being*. After a few months, he reported he was now the "guru" of his gym and could beat all the other fighters there. After that, I started to teach him how to fight.

Although there is a lot of work to be done, with all that has been outlined so far and what still remains to be shared, the best approach is probably to be excited every step of the way as you learn and investigate, making it a fun adventure rather than a dull procedure. This way, you're far more likely to put in the time and effort while enhancing your life experience throughout.

FOUNDATION SKILLS FOR POWERFUL OPERATING PRINCIPLES

Having trained your body, mind, and perceptions in the distinctions that I have elaborated so far, you have much of what it takes to interact effectively. You now know that if your experience is designed, or redesigned, so that it accurately reflects what's going on, your actions will relate to what's occurring. If you make the necessary distinctions that provide for a constant determination of what's appropriate, your actions will be effective. Yet the task of putting all of this information into action is considerable. To do that, you need to understand the principles and states that make it possible.

You've seen the need to translate all incoming perceptive data into one feeling-sense. Yet what principles can assist in finding and building this sophisticated feeling-intelligence? One thing you need in your pursuit is a direction for action that is simple yet draws you to discover all of the distinctions and their appropriate applications in each circumstance. This should be a goal that will keep your actions open to correction and moving toward mastery. Like I proposed earlier, one possible principle that fulfills this requirement is the effortless principle.

When you've managed to improve the operations of your own body and mind, you can turn your attention to principles that improve your level of skill. Interactive skill with others is found in how well you perform in relation to the activity of others. Here you need to find principles behind being effective in your field so that an interaction turns to your advantage, and possibly to the advantage of all involved. If there are no other people involved, then turn attention onto the circumstances or objects with which you interact.

Toward that end, I want to draw your attention to three useful principles in order to provide a skeleton upon which to begin hanging and incorporating the immense amount of information that you have compiled. Obviously, your effectiveness in an interaction is determined by your ability to interact—with people, objects, or environment. Your ability to interact is greatly enhanced when determined by an effective operating principle that provides the context for your actions. To be effective it must generate not only responsive action, but appropriately responsive action that is designed to be advantageous.

In order to ensure that your actions are arising in relation to the relevant occurring activities, you need for your impulses and actions to be governed by a principle that demands, as well as ensures, that this is the case. One of the most universal principles that accomplishes this is "following," a term that can apply to many different forms and methods of accomplishing this principle and other similar principles. The general principle involves taking action solely and always in relation to the action of another or event, moving in sync with what's occurring.

To embody any form of the governing principles of following, joining, inclusion, communication, and so on, another principle we could call "listening" is essential. Without this ability, those other principles are not possible. If understood properly, your pursuit is further empowered with two more abilities I call "outreaching" and "yielding." These foundational abilities are predecessors to a bunch of very powerful interactive operating principles that we'll look at later. As I elaborate on each, look into them and consider how they can be applied to your field.

Listening

"Listening" is a great perceptive ability. It is activating a high level of sensitive feeling-awareness of what's happening in the moment. Listening is what puts you in touch, and keeps you in touch, with what's occurring. Primarily, it's understanding what's taking place on the other side of an interaction or an activity or object.

Listening may be the foremost ingredient in any relationship that turns out well. To listen is to know what's there. Although listening is often seen as focusing on another person's experience via their speaking, it can also be applied to an object by feeling for (or "listening to") the feedback the object provides as you interact with it. In relation to another's experience, listening is not making a judgment about them, or figuring out what may be going on with them, nor is it anticipating what they might do or say. It is actually being with them and being open to them, without the filters of "useful" or "dangerous" influencing what is received as their experience, intent, or actions.

If listening is held as something to exclusively serve your demands or needs, or if it is influenced by your reactions or biases, it will not function as it does when unhampered, and so it will not actually be the principle I'm calling listening. To have power, its service to you can only be determined after the fact. Attempting to predetermine what you want to be there, or what you fear may be there, or applying any value to what is received beyond its mere existence is to displace listening in that moment. Therefore, any evaluation of usefulness must be reserved as a separate and independent activity for another time. In other words, you need to get what is going on as it is without relating it to your self-concerns, even though you will be relating what's there to your objectives in the same moment.

Listening is the same as actually "hearing" what someone says. In other words, not just hearing the words or merely understanding the meaning of a sentence, but grasping the *experience* the other is communicating. In physical interactions, it is just as important to listen. This takes the form of focusing on the current activity and getting it as it is without bias or reaction. It includes being sensitive to and aware of all that is felt, done, thought, or perceived by another. This is received as a sensitive feeling-experience of the other or an object, keeping you in touch with what is actually going on so you can relate to what's occurring and not to your own reactions, projections, imagination, concepts, plans, and so on. This is a skill.

In some ways, it's like a safecracker "listening" to the feeling of the tumblers as he works to open the safe. He has to reach out with his feeling and attention and "hear" what is happening inside the safe. This is a form of listening. This kind of listening also applies to objects. When playing with a sword, for example, I feel the whole object, including the center of its mass where managing it is most effective. As I "listen" to (feel) the sword's weight, shape, and motion, this provides feedback about how the sword "wants" to move and be moved to operate most effectively. From this feedback, sword mastery becomes possible.

Within listening there is an inherent sense of connection and responsiveness to what's received. As this ability develops, one can learn to respond to another's intent without intellectually categorizing what is sensed. The link between listening and responding can become so direct, and free of any other associated activity, that it is only intellectually recognized as having occurred after the fact. At this stage, listening's effectiveness is not determined by your normal self-mind because it occurs prior to the mental and emotional self-referencing that exists to serve a personal agenda.

Listening is to be found in the very obvious, the very near, and the very person or condition that is right in front of you. In other words, what is simply there. You shouldn't confuse taken-for-granted projections filled with personal assumptions and knee-jerk conclusions with listening. It's not the same thing. The former is just the mind's automatic filling-in-the-blanks of what you assume is going on.

On the other hand, if you hold listening as mysterious, or as something very subtle, you can get lost in intellect and abstraction and fall into the trap of searching but not finding. Frequently, I say to people: "Find. Don't just search." When someone is working with me, going through the motions of listening but not actually "hearing" me or getting in touch with me, I often say "Here I am!" and show them that I am the one he or she needs to be listening to, rather than some notion about listening. The concept of listening is only a function of one's own mind and not a function of the *principle* or activity of listening.

Although I am describing these principles in stages, they actually all occur in each moment. I am making these distinctions for the purpose of study and development. The experience may be quite different from any conclusion or image you have while considering what I'm saying. Once you create this experience, however, it will match the descriptions that I've made. Even though they match, there is still a danger. The danger lies in the fact that they do match.

If you fail to make a distinction between the present experience actually taking place, and the idea or concept of the experience, then in your endeavor you are apt to try to reproduce the concept and not the principle. Of course, this won't work very well. This often goes unnoticed and can occur in the midst of an activity. You should search out and develop a real capacity to notice when a principle is actively being lived or is just a concept that you're holding.

For example, long ago, when I was trying to develop a powerful but effortless punch, I learned something even more valuable than the punch. Using a very large 110-pound bag hanging from a branch in the backyard, my goal was to hit the bag so that it swung high enough to touch another branch about the same height as the one from which it was hanging. This would make the bag a bit less than parallel to the ground. As you might imagine, this was a difficult task—and remember, my goal was to do this without the use of muscular strength. I experimented a lot, and invented ways to go about accomplishing this task, many of which involved serious mind control. Eventually I was successful, but I learned a very important lesson.

The first time I managed to successfully hit the bag so that it flew away like never before, I was thrilled. Then, of course, I tried to repeat this action. But I failed. I was surprised it didn't work, because I had just done it. Why couldn't I repeat the very same feat? As I studied this, I discovered the reason I failed the second time was I was trying to repeat the *concept* of what I'd done, not the experience that led to success the first time. The first time, I had no concept of how it would go or whether it would be successful. My attention was on questioning and feeling and doing those things I had invented—which required a very different state of mind, complex alignments, mental control, and precise actions.

So by trying to reproduce the concept or memory of the result, I failed miserably. Once I put myself back into the state and experience I was in the first time, it worked again. This was a great lesson. Rather than trying to reproduce the concept of a result, I learned to engage the process that created the result. These two things are very different. Clearly, this point relates to far more than listening, so it is important to get that all these principles and skills only work if you *do* them, not just *know* them. Also, like I mentioned, you can easily slip into the concept of listening and not actually listen. It's wise to be alert for that happening when training any of these principles.

Outreaching

Outreaching is a link between listening and action. I use the term "outreach" to refer to personally making a feeling-connection with whatever is occurring. When listening is taking place, the first element of outreaching has occurred. You then "reach out" with your feeling-attention to "touch" or "connect" with the other person or object. When you make a feeling-connection with every part of an object or another's mind, whole body, and actions, then you are outreaching.

In a physical endeavor this can be done with or without physical touch. If an object is involved, like a golf club or a ball, feel and connect with the entire object, as if reaching your feeling-awareness into every part of the whole object. In an interactive, physical-contact sport, your goal is to connect with another's whole body. When you can feel every part of his or her whole body through, but not limited to, the part with which you're making contact, then you are outreaching. In nonphysical interactions, this is done through a focus of attention and awareness on the other or activity, not interfering in any way with what is there, but instead connecting with them or it. When involved in an activity, you must continue to outreach and stay connected to the whole, no matter what changes may come about.

Practice and improve your outreaching ability in your field. If you are always in touch with ("listening") and *connected* to every part of the activity taking place, or the object or body, then you are outreaching. Remember, mastery arises only through the principles by which effective and precisely appropriate interaction can take place. These principles are not added to or just steps to mastery; they are inherent in it.

Yielding

One often overlooked principle in mastery is knowing when to yield. In order to yield, however, you should understand the principle. An integral aspect of yielding is the ability to let go. This skill can be applied broadly to many domains and activities, from relaxing to letting go of a belief or a plan. As with all principles, people frequently mistake the method or idea with the principle. Yielding is simply neutralizing any encountered forces or actions that are inappropriate or would put you at a disadvantage or harm you or your efforts in some way. This also applies to letting go of any activities you are undertaking that are inappropriate or ineffective.

When you are aligned with the principles that make up being effective, your natural state will likely be balanced, whole, and centered, as well as connected, sensitive, and aware. This condition could be called a balanced state. However, whenever an action is taken—whether generated by you or encountered by you—this balance is immediately threatened. Therefore, as you act, you must constantly include and relate to the forces that act upon you in order to maintain your balance—physically, mentally, or socially.

Yielding to any incoming force is most often an appropriate response. In this case, the principle is not to succumb or be dominated by the force, but to neutralize it, to make it impotent and take away its power. This keeps you in balance and capable of responding. Yielding and letting go should remain at the top of the list of active principles since they allow you access to other, even more powerful principles of interaction.

Yielding takes away the opportunity for another person or situation to use force against you, disrupt you, or take advantage of you in some way. It also affords the opportunity to drop your own activities that limit or disrupt your efforts. In this way, you remain balanced. It is worth contemplating the nature of this. When there is no activity, balance is a natural element of one's condition. Standing on the train tracks, you might be balanced, but when a train comes, if you remain, you will not be balanced or alive for long. Stepping off the tracks allows you to remain whole and balanced and in control of your body. When the disruptive or unwanted aspects of an activity are neutralized through yielding in some fashion, balance can be maintained. The state of mind in which this principle can operate most effectively is one that I call being "calm and present."

Many people seem to have difficulty remaining calm or present, especially when attempting to accomplish something or engaging a difficult endeavor. But to stay calm and present is neither extraordinary nor difficult. It's a bit like water flowing downhill; it quite naturally occurs without effort as long as it's allowed to be water. If you're trying to get water to flow uphill, then it becomes an effort and a problem. Similarly, being calm is simply allowing the experience of "now" to be as it is, rather than being disturbed by it, and being present is simply attending to it. What would it look like to apply the principles of yielding, as well as calmness and presence, to your field?

The principles of listening, outreaching, and yielding, as well as calmness and presence, provide a base upon which you can create even more powerful principles to assist you in obtaining mastery. Listening provides the accurate and unvarnished experience of what's there, what's occurring. Outreaching keeps you mentally and physically connected and responsive to what's there. And yielding keeps you balanced by neutralizing influencing forces and allows you to act effectively and powerfully. It is also consistent with the principle of effortlessness. When these principles are active, you are in a position to take on more specific operating principles that make it easier for you to create mastery.

POWERFUL INTERACTIVE OPERATING PRINCIPLES

As we've seen, in the principle of effective interaction: *your actions need to relate appropriately to the occurring event so that the purpose for the interaction is realized.* But this sounds rather abstract and is certainly general, so to help ground it, let's look into principles for interaction that are more specific and contain elements that serve to direct your actions in ways consistent with this general principle. These operating principles make mastery much more likely.

We've seen that outreaching provides a connection with the occurring activity but that staying with and responding to each aspect of the process is necessary in order to keep that connection. This is called following. I introduced following earlier, but now let's look into it in more detail, along with several other companion principles that are all worth gold when it comes to pursuing mastery—especially in interactive endeavors. In more sedentary fields you'll have to adapt them in whatever ways work best for you.

There are many interactive principles that make a huge difference in effectiveness. In order to work, however, they must become the central governing principles for your relating. They must influence perceptive-interpretation, design your strategies, and direct your actions. Consistent with following, eight other principles that produce appropriately commensurate action are: joining, complementing, leading, cutting, sprouting, borrowing, choiceless, and changing. Some of these principles apply only to fields that relate to other people, but all will have to be adapted to your particular field, no matter what it is.

These aren't the only possible principles—you could create more—but for most people, these nine principles are far more than they will ever need. In your field, you may not find some of these principles as effective as they might be in other fields, but through their study you can glean the central elements that make them powerful, and can choose, determine, or invent other principles that work best in your field.

Adhering to any one of these principles ensures that your actions are completely designed by the actions and intent of the other or event. The names themselves give you an idea of the principle behind the activity (although some will need considerably more clarification). Still, exercise your creative thinking for each one and consider: What actually *is* the principle? What is the experience of the underlying principle behind every one of these methods for interaction? Also, imagine the state of mind that would be necessary to make it real. Whatever each principle is, understanding it and adhering to it should be your primary concern in bringing about effective interaction. Within such a principle—and in developing the experiential skills outlined so far—any action you take will appropriately relate to the occurring event.

Before I begin describing these principles, I want to offer a word of caution. I've been teaching for a very long time and have worked with many thousands of people. One thing I've noticed is that the majority of those introduced to any principle, and certainly these principles, fail to actually experience them and are unable to put them to use as well as they should. Hearing about them, and even witnessing them being demonstrated repeatedly, isn't enough. I think a possible reason for this is that people have a hard time creating a reality that is different from the one they already have in place, but it can be done. Many times, it seems they don't know the difference between the conceptual understanding of something and the experience of it.

As you read on, know that a given principle won't be truly useful, or help you, unless you can take it into action, and have it apply to more than your intellect. It may be useful to note that these principles have mostly been unknown, even to people of advanced studies in applicable arts. In the martial world, for example, historically any one of these would have been kept a secret and shared only with very few top and deserving students—that is, if the teacher even knew them—and most arts do not have any of them. I am trying to impress upon you the profundity of these principles and what a privilege it is for you to have access to them.

Over half of the following principles have been invented by me, and those that were taught to me were taken to a greater depth and to a wider field of application. I don't mind sharing everything I know at this point. But try not to be one of those people who will fail to grasp them for real. Apparently, the best "hiding" place is the middle of the floor. The overlooked obvious prevents most of us from experiencing the principles for what they are. So don't overlook the obvious, and do be sure to put these principles to work—effortlessly, of course.

Penetrating what is overlooked, even if it seems obvious, to grasp what is really going on is needed if you're going to make use of these principles as powerfully as I have. You need to perceive the occurring activity in relation to the principle, and "feel" it actually moving your actions in response, thus manifesting the principle. Your state of mind and disposition *must* be aligned with and dominated by the principle. For them to work, you have to surrender to the principle and throw yourself into an experience that manifests it in each and every moment of engagement. Do these things and the principle will bring you to mastery.

Following

Stick to the activity like glue.

"Following" is commensurately matching the activity that is taking place with your own actions. There are many ways to follow, but in each your actions are dictated solely by the activity that is occurring. Put simply, if something goes up you go up; if action goes left you follow left. You stick to every action like glue, staying with it, moving in sync with it. You don't necessarily have to mirror what is being done—in other words, doing the exact same thing in the same way—but you must respond to everything done by moving *with* it, rather than acting against it, being stagnant, or lagging behind.

It's a little like an episode that happened in ancient China during a famous Go match. A seemingly unbeatable Go master was competing against someone far less skilled. The lesser player knew that he couldn't beat the master, and so he simply matched the master move for move. Each time the master played a stone, his opponent made the exact same move throughout the game. Unexpectedly, the less skilled player actually won the match. You can see that by following, you would be very close to the level of skill of the other person, because you would be doing the same thing he is doing, as he does it. Of course, you will intend to turn following to your advantage, but it starts, and remains, with this same basic idea.

This principle is not about following later, meaning you don't follow by responding after the fact, but at the same time. Following—like all of the principles addressed here—forces you to pay very close attention to and be governed by whatever is occurring. How could you follow if you didn't know what was happening in every moment? You couldn't. If you were a detective trying to follow someone, you would be unable to do so unless you knew exactly where the person was at all times; this then dictates your actions. You can't follow without constantly knowing what's happening in present time.

Following also keeps you constantly in touch with and responding to what's happening, since being presently aware and responsive are inherent in the principle. Knowing what is occurring and being responsive to each and every thing that is occurring are worth gold because of the principle of effective interaction. Following provides those elements without fail—otherwise, you're not following.

While you follow, always remain in sync and in harmony with the forces and activities that are occurring, and adjust the relationship to take advantage of what's going on, using it to accomplish your goals and objectives. Accomplishing your goals must always be done within the context of following. If you stop following in order to try to accomplish something, you'll break the connection and will get into trouble. Everything you accomplish must be done *while* you follow. If something can't be done while following then don't do it, and instead look for another opportunity.

Adhering to any of these interactive principles accomplishes so much of what we've discussed that is necessary for mastery—and this is true just by focusing on one principle. With the strong foundation built through the work done so far, when you are engaged in the principle of following, almost everything you need for mastery takes place.

While you are following, the only other ingredient you need is to find ways to make things turn out as you want. It becomes very difficult for you to fail or get into trouble because you are always moving *with* the action and so forces can't be successfully applied against you. As you can see, yielding is inherent in following because when some force is moving your way you must move with it in order to follow. This is the same as yielding. When an opportunity presents itself, you are already right there to take advantage. If you aren't following, you will have to cover ground or try to catch up, and by that time the situation may well have changed, and the opportunity may have passed.

Are you grasping the principle here? In your field, how can you apply this principle? You may have to work out details that are applicable to your field before you can successfully apply it, but when you do, it will become easy and your skill will leap ahead to a new level.

Joining

Merge with and contribute to the
activity to take it over.

"Joining" is what it sounds like. It is joining with the activity of another or with whatever is happening—becoming one with it, so to speak. It is similar to and founded on following, since all of your actions must be based on the actions and intent of the other or event. Once you are connected with and a part of the activity that is taking place, you can then contribute to it in such a way that you redirect that activity to serve your objectives. Once you join with what's there, you can take over, because you are part of it; you are doing it.

As with following, joining can only occur after outreaching has been accomplished. In order to join, of course, you need listening to know what's there, and outreaching to maintain a connection to and an appropriate relationship with what's there. You can then join and contribute to and take control of the activity. You don't resist anything, you simply redirect it. Within this context, any result produced on your part will be "joining."

Joining is akin to a river merging with another river. As a river, you'd first come around to move parallel to and then flow into the other river. Coming together in this way, both rivers are now pushing in the same direction. Once you are flowing in the same direction as the other river, you can contribute to the merged rivers flowing in a new direction. Although you are adding your energy and contributing to the flow, this is done without strain or fighting the other river, because it is also going in the same direction. You simply help that flow move in a slightly different direction that serves your objectives.

As we've already seen in other foundational principles, joining—

like all of these operating principles—requires balance. Balance is accomplished by neutralizing any forces, pressures, and activities that influence your ability to effectively relate to the interaction. When listening, outreaching, and balance are a constant, you can then follow and "join" whatever is there in its activity.

When you think of creating a result through a volitional act, however, you immediately run into a danger. You've seen the danger of leaving behind the principle of interaction and pursuing activity focused solely on accomplishing a desired end. This is a danger because a myopic focus on the desired result may well override clear and open inclusion of the real condition of the moment. You will impose actions upon whatever is happening, trying to attain a result, to the detriment of the principle.

This is not dangerous because it is "bad" but because it doesn't truly work. The danger appears all the more ominous when you recognize that a temporary and partial—almost always effortful—attempt to get something to work out in the short run obscures the fact that this very activity will often be the source of many of your upcoming problems. What you don't see is that this approach has not worked in a broader sense. Nor do you see that the effort and problems that frequently arise—which you may overcome by force or luck—are a result of the very nature of this way of interacting and so are not resolvable within the same dynamic.

Although you pursue results consistent with your objectives, remember that results are only a part of a larger process. The exclusive pursuit of a result creates a dynamic of relationship that, by its very nature, supports the myth that results are a sole function of effort and willfully imposed manipulation. It also supports the notion that the ultimate end or zenith to mastery is to get to do what you want, and to do it your way. Since you may be accustomed to this way of thinking, feeling, and acting, to think in any other way will appear contrary to many of the automatic impulses that you have. The principle of joining helps to avoid this pitfall.

Joining demands a different state of mind from the ones you probably automatically frequent. Joining is not exclusively a pursuit of
attaining desired results. The principle of joining is steeped in inclusion
and involvement with every part of the process that arises. If others are
involved, you are helping them do whatever they are doing: you are not
fighting or resisting them; you are joining the action. It is the same with
an object: you don't fight it; you join it and its demands.

Remember, in order to join, it is essential that in your mind and your
actions you don't resist what's occurring but completely include, accept,
and merge with it. Once you have joined the efforts of others or the activity at hand, you will be "inside" it, so to speak, and since you are participating in doing it, you can contribute to what's occurring. Only then can
you redirect the flow or direction to serve your objectives. It's like joining
a group. Once you are contributing to the group's efforts, you can start
to channel them in certain directions because you are part of the group.

Each interaction has to be related to on its own terms. If people
are involved, these things can only be determined by listening to the
intentions and actions of others. Sacrifice your own desires and will to
include theirs, and join them in their efforts. What's also true is that
you aren't doing this for them. It is what allows you to remain inclusive
of conditions and so be effective.

If you're relating to an event or object, whatever is occurring or
present can be joined. You have to work out how to do that, but it starts
with adopting a feeling-disposition of joining whatever is there. In spe-
cialized circumstances, such as playing a game or sport, in business, or
in some other matter, the dynamic and principle of joining is the same,
but the form will be different. A game exists as a match or recreation
in which agreements are made, and from these agreements the actions
of the relationship are determined. Business often involves conflicting
interests that must be managed. In essence, blend with and follow the
activity or forces involved, and as you do, contribute your own actions
to turn the activity in your favor.

Joining also works with activities of your own mind, such as drives, thoughts, or emotions that you find unhealthy, or ineffective, or that get in the way of being appropriate to your current task. One's first reaction is usually to resist such experiences, or get swept away by them, neither of which works very well. Entering a struggle against something you're doing is fundamentally an unsound strategy. Instead, it is far more effective to join the activity.

For example, say you have an emotion that you'd rather not have. If you direct your feeling-attention to merge with and join this emotion—not judging it or resisting it, or feeling overwhelmed by it—you move into the position of *doing* it, and being responsible for doing it. You become aligned with it in your experience and mind—because you *are* doing it and you *are* responsible for it. Once that is the case, you find that you can change it or stop doing it. This is the power of joining.

Can you see how to apply this principle to whatever you do?

Complementing

Shape your actions around arising actions.

"Complementing" is also a form of following. This basic principle is to act in a complementary fashion to whatever action arises. Just as the shape of one spoon fits exactly onto the shape of another spoon, you shape your actions to complement the other's actions. It is consistent with the following statement: "When a force comes to my left, I empty my left and fill the right." In a martial context, as the opponent takes actions, you mold your body around those actions, emptying where he is solid and filling in where he is empty. In other words, dodging or yielding to his attack while going around the attack, complementing it with your own attack at the very same time.

Whenever something takes shape, either physically or conceptually, it has direction and form. This could be a movement or an activity, assertion or line of thinking, or a process or transaction. Whatever the form is, complement that form with your own form that fits it like a glove. Note that the glove may complement the hand but is shaped around the hand. It's not shaped *as* a hand but *by* the hand.

How does complementing assist you in being effective? First, it establishes the "golden rule" of all these principles: it forces you to constantly focus your attention on the occurring activity, without which you could not proceed to complement the activity. The principle further demands that you constantly respond to every action or process in such a way that you maintain a commensurate relationship with it. In this way, anything that puts you at a disadvantage is immediately neutralized by virtue of the principle itself.

Given this relationship, you can proceed to arrange your actions to serve your objectives and turn activities to your advantage. This last point is clearly a very important ingredient, but adhering to the principle leaves you with a very small gap to cover to reach mastery. With the distinctions you've made, and the recognition of how any current activity relates to your objective, it becomes obvious how to apply this advantageous or appropriate ingredient. Also, the need for convoluted strategies is reduced remarkably because most of your strategy is devoted to merely adhering to the principle. Once there, you have few strategic decisions to make. The simple profundity of such principles provides you with sophisticated strategic possibilities.

Of course, you will have to work out how such a relationship looks in your field of study. In some domains, you will have to ponder what the "shape" or direction of the activity is that you must complement. Then, contemplate how you can complement it. What do you need to do or how do you need to be so that you can mold your actions around whatever arises in a complementary fashion?

When you interlace the fingers of both hands, they fit in a complementary fashion, and both hands are in the same basic condition. One hand can't do anything radically different from the other, so the hands are brought to a common situation. From here it is impossible to take advantage of one hand without the other knowing about the attempt. Like following or joining, once you match the activity by complementing, you can turn things toward accomplishing your objectives. Even if you end up rarely using this principle in your field, the task of working out how to do it will teach you a great deal about your own endeavor and open your mind to new possibilities and insights.

Leading

Offer what is desired to draw another's actions
and take control of them.

"Leading" only relates to interactions with living creatures. You should be able to see a commonality to following, joining, and complementing. With the jump to "leading," you may not see the connection. But the truth is, leading is also a form of following. You can't lead without being constantly in touch with and relating to what's occurring. In this way, you must follow the intent and actions of others in order to lead them.

Every action a person—or another living creature—takes is based on a desire for something to happen. This desire forms into an intent, and then action is taken to obtain a result. The essential factors to leading that need to occur for those being led are:

1. Desire and intent
2. The perception of the possible availability of what's desired, and
3. Action to obtain what's desired

For example, if I want to lead a horse into a barn, I might offer him an apple. The horse needs to desire the apple; otherwise, this won't work. If I offer him a tin can, he is likely to ignore it. So, recognizing and presenting what the other wants is the first ingredient.

Also, the horse must perceive the apple. If I keep it hidden, he will have no intent to get it. When I present the apple to the horse, two things need to occur. One, he needs to perceive it—in this case, see and smell it. Two, even though he can't get it, he must see it as available—generating the intent to get it to fulfill his desire.

But if I give him the apple he will stay where he is and not follow me. So, I must make it available without letting him get it. If I keep the apple just out of reach, the horse will take a step forward to eat it. As he moves, I will step back, and so on. I walk into the barn with the apple always available but just out of reach. When I get him in the barn I can give him the apple (after all, I'm not a monster!) and close the door. Voila! The horse has been led into the barn.

Leading can be applied to any activity. As long as someone wants something, they can be led. This can apply to conversation, business, personal relating, fighting, sports, or what have you. For example, if I'm holding a target and you want to shoot an arrow into it, you must point your arrow toward the target. If I move the target to the right, you are required to point your arrow to the right. So, I can lead your movement by moving the target toward a desired result.

You might ask: What could I accomplish moving the target like that? Perhaps I want you to shoot the evil, fire-breathing dragon hiding in the bushes, and so by moving the target I lead your arrow to point toward him—and then when you loose the arrow I suddenly drop the target and you hit the dragon. Or perhaps I don't want you to put holes in my new target, and so moving it to the right forces you to change your aim to the right, and as you shoot I move it to the left so you miss the target. This happens because you must follow the extrapolation of the moving target in order to hit it when it's moving—but when you commit to the act, if I change direction at the right time, you must miss it.

In every activity that involves people, there will be a desire for something to occur. Offer this to them, make it available but not yet gotten, and as they take action to obtain it, move or change just enough to control the direction of the unfolding action so that they perceive they can get what they want if they just do such and such. In this way, you control their actions and can produce results favorable to your objectives.

In bullfighting, the matador is the target, and he uses the solid looking object of a cape to attract the bull who just wants to charge something. As the bull starts to bury his head near the cape, the matador moves the cape in front of the bull, leading him to one side as the matador moves to the other. Head to head the matador would stand no chance against the weight, strength, and horns of the bull. He cannot resist the bull or block him. But he can lead the bull's mind. All that tonnage of mass and muscle is safely led to one side because where the bull's desire and perception are led, the body must follow.

One of the distinctions you need to be sensitive to in leading—as well as in the other interactive principles—is to be able to read the other's intent. I've mentioned an example of this—when I demonstrate having someone sit on a chair—but let's revisit and expand your understanding of reading intent using this example once again.

Standing behind my volunteer, I will ask them to sit in a chair. I have them do this a couple times. Then, as they begin to sit, I wait until I sense they have made the commitment to put their weight onto the chair. This occurs just before they touch it, because they must shift from lowering their body to relaxing the legs and allowing the chair to take their weight. At this moment, if I pull the chair away, they will fall down to the floor.

To make it even clearer, I will ask them to look between their legs as they sit. When they do this, I will pull the chair away before they've committed to sit, and of course they will not sit. Then we will repeat, and I let them sit. Often, they become gun-shy and don't want to commit, but moving the body downward and sitting are two different things. They'll bounce their ass off the chair a few times until they settle down to sit.

Once their brain is adjusted to sitting again, even as they watch the chair between their legs, when I sense their intent to sit and pull the chair away, they still fall down. Knowing doesn't change anything. Their actions are subject to the laws of intent and action, and if they commit to sit, they will sit. At that moment, if there is no chair, there is also no going back, and they will sit on the floor. Although this example is about reading intent rather than leading, it clearly illustrates the skill of reading intent, which must be a part of leading, as well as part of other principles on this list.

In leading, you must stay in touch with the other's mind. Sense what they perceive, their desire, and what they intend to do about it in order to lead their mind and so lead their actions. If at any point they change any of it, you must also change to lead what they desire, perceive, and intend now. Staying current gives you the power to stay in control of the outcomes.

Leading, like all the other principles, must be a constant activity, not a technique. This seems to be especially difficult for people to get. Most people will always try to do it as a technique to be applied when they think about it. This won't be very effective because, like I've said, the relationship is ongoing, and your effectiveness depends on seamlessly and constantly abiding in the principle.

Like the other principles, if it's to be effective, you must surrender to the principle of leading, allowing it to dominate your mind and actions. In this way, the bulk of your strategy is handled, and your actions will always be in touch with and responsive to what's occurring. Again, from here turning it to your advantage is not difficult, because you're already in control of the activity. You can influence, and to a degree control, the actions of others and direct these actions to your benefit. But you must surrender to the principle and allow it to govern your actions. Then it is guaranteed to work, just like in the chair demonstration, where the sitter is guaranteed to sit when the proper conditions are met.

How can you apply leading to your field?

Cutting

Reduce the potential for disruptive action to
take shape; and don't fall behind.

"Cutting" is an unusual name and requires explanation—any more accurate or revealing name would actually be a sentence. Cutting refers to reducing or eliminating the potential for something to occur. The potential we usually want to reduce is whatever would put us in a bad place or in some kind of danger or disadvantage, but it can be applied to anything. There are conditions that have to be met for anything to occur. We've talked about a few: perception, intent, action, structure, process, and the condition of the relationship in any given moment. As I mentioned, anytime we can read another's intent, we will know what they are going to do. But there is more.

For some result to take place, the structure and movement of the activity must align in specific ways so that the result can be realized. For example, say you want to thrust a spear into my body. In order to do that, you need to position your body close enough to reach me with the spear, but not so close you can't fit the spear in the space between us. You also have to align the spear to point toward my body and align your body behind the spear to give it thrust and power. All of these conditions need to be met for you to accomplish this result.

But I'm not stationary. If I move my body too close to you, there is not enough space for the spear. If I move to the side of the spear so the tip of the spear is pointing at space, you cannot thrust it in me. You may be able to try and impale me with the side of the spearhead, but depending on how I move, I can cut that too. Even if you can manage to get some cut by twisting your body in a way that is not well-aligned to the task, it will still not have the power or effectiveness of the thrust, and so I have "cut" or reduced what you can do. There are many possible adjustments on my part that can disrupt your ability to either accomplish your result or reduce the effectiveness of any result you may accomplish.

This is true of any interaction and most activities. Recognize the conditions that are necessary for something to be done, and ask what action you can take *before* any action can be taken to make the conditions necessary to do it inappropriate or ineffective. When relating to another person, if or when they notice your adjustment and readjust *their* actions because they are still trying to accomplish a result, you adjust again, and then again if needed, staying constantly prior to any attempt they can make. As you maintain this relationship, making it impossible for them to mount or complete any effective process, you can then take actions to accomplish your goals while they are in a disempowered condition. Cutting fits well with the principle of "not falling behind."

In cutting, you learn to act *before* something happens. You take action in relation to the *potential* for something to happen. It's similar to an action in the movie *The Seven Samurai.* In one scene, the collected samurai are sitting in a room facing toward the door. One of the samurai—played by an actor who was the only one with actual sword skill—has his sword on the mat to the side of his body nearest the door. Toshiro Mifune, the undisciplined Samurai want-to-be, comes in drunk and raucous, acting erratically. Our kneeling samurai picks up his sword, switches it to his other side and behind him, out of the way, thus avoiding a possible mishap. Then, a bit later, when the opportunity presents itself, he picks up Mifune's sword—which Mifune put down to unravel a scroll in an attempt to prove he was a samurai—and quickly passes it behind him to another samurai, again avoiding a future problem. This is taking action before it is needed to prevent something that could happen. Are you getting the picture?

Cutting is a sister principle to leading. Both manage the unfolding process and control activity by taking action prior to the possibility of an unwanted result. Leading acts on the intent and potential of another, using their desire by offering a perceived opportunity to attract their action but then draw it in directions that serve your goals. In this way, you control their actions. On the other hand, cutting acts on this same potential, but destroys its effectiveness. Rather than presenting a target or opportunity—as in leading—you take it away, either doing this visibly to prevent some action, or intending for it to go unnoticed so that you can take advantage of a subsequent action by another. Either way, you control activity by managing potential.

Go over typical scenarios of how things have unfolded in the past in your field. Isolate the conditions that had to be met for a given situation to turn out the way it did. Study those times you were ineffective. What happened before negative results began to appear? Clarify the conditions that led to these results before they happened, isolating the very beginning of their potential to happen. Notice what you perceived before action was taken about the potential for action.

Now, ask yourself what you could have done early on to alter what could happen so that you would have been successful. When you've considered one scenario, think through another. When you've evaluated a healthy cross section of every probable scenario you're likely to encounter, you should have a good idea of what actions to take to align to the principle of cutting. Try to get a feel for the experience that would arise in order to be successful at doing what I describe. Then take it into action. Engage your endeavor and make cutting your operating principle. Remember, make it a constant and pursue your goals only while cutting is happening, and you will be on top of the situation.

Sprouting

Nip unwanted activity in the bud.

Another principle with an unusual name—this time, more poetic than descriptive—requires clarification. "Sprouting" refers to the earliest moment a process begins, at the conception and intent stage. This principle requires a very sensitive faculty of picking up on the moment someone creates the intent to act or the conditions are met for some activity to begin. Recall the demonstration of pulling the chair out from under someone. This is the kind of faculty you need for sprouting. Your actions will relate to this inception point where you handle and shut down any action that does not serve your ends before it arises.

You may be wondering how this differs from cutting. As with all of these principles, they have aspects in common. In this case, however, you aren't reducing or eliminating potential for action by adjusting the conditions necessary to make it work; you are destroying the action itself before it begins. In some ways, it's like destroying the oak seed before it even falls to the ground, so it can't begin to grow into a tree. In this metaphor, the seed represents the mere idea or intent to do something, and the tree is something you don't want to happen.

When I was just a boy of about six, I would get into fights with my older brother. In those days, the mid-fifties, there was an honor code that you couldn't hit someone until they hit you first. This didn't make sense to me since I had to get hit before I could attack back. So I changed the rule; I said that one can attack if the other even thinks about or intends to hit. My brother agreed and this became the new rule. Sprouting is a bit like that, except the sense needed is even deeper than what I could pick up on as a child—or maybe not.

As you take action to interrupt the process at the intent or inception stage, you do so by creating your own action to produce results that at the same time destroy or negate adverse activity. You take action that eliminates a process that you don't want to occur at its inception point. With sprouting, you relate to the very first glimpse of the origins of any activity. At this place, you can nip the action in the bud.

As with all of these principles, keep sprouting constantly active throughout the endeavor. Always remain ahead of any intended action or preparation, and manage the relationship from this place. Can you perceive the inception point of any activity that will arise in your field? How could you relate to this moment to create your own actions that negate the arising of difficult circumstances while at the same time producing favorable results for you?

Borrowing

Absorb incoming forces and cycle them back
to the source.

"Borrowing" is what it sounds like. Yet it can be difficult to imagine how this could occur in ways other than borrowing money or a hammer or something similar. Here, you borrow the activity or energy or force of a process to use for your own actions. This does take skill.

In a physical context, a movement or pressure that is applied can be absorbed and cycled back. It is used to fuel your own actions to turn the force back toward its source. In a nonphysical context, it would take a different form. Certainly, you could borrow another's idea to use as your own, but that might be more like stealing. But consider a way to use the force of the idea to fuel your own success, or cycle it back to the source if that serves your ends.

In a simplistic sense, if a force were applied to your body, instead of resisting the force or being disturbed by it, you use this force to move your own body in some way advantageous to you. In a more sophisticated sense, if someone blocks your attack, you absorb the force of the block to move your whole body so as to compress into the ground and spring it back to the source—or you cycle the block around using your opponent's energy to attack them with it. Using a force is very different than fighting it or succumbing to it.

I once read a book about Herman Melville's life, and he recounted a story at sea where he ran into a frightening storm that produced huge waves. Most of the crew were scared to death and worried the boat would be overwhelmed. A couple of Hawaiian natives, who'd also signed on to crew the ship, jumped into the water and road the waves, surfing them and having fun! The same circumstance produced very different experiences, depending on how one related to it, didn't it? One resisted the waves, at least mentally, while the other borrowed the power of the waves for their own recreation.

Whatever comes at you, use it and cycle it back in a way that serves your objective. You might also give it back with "interest." In a physical sense, borrowing takes specific learned skills too involved to tackle here—you'll have to invent your own. In other fields, consider what activities or forces are involved in your endeavor and how they influence you or your objectives. Then contemplate how you can use these influences, allowing them to arise but adjusting your relationship to them so that you can use their energy to fuel your own actions that turn or cycle these forces back to the source, influencing the endeavor as a whole. Can you create a way to do that in your field?

EVEN MORE ADVANCED PRINCIPLES

Although all of these principles are very advanced, the last two I will introduce are even more innovative and challenging to grasp. They might appear more abstract and difficult to understand than the others because the principles are based on distinctions not as easily perceived. But trust me, they are powerful.

Choiceless

*In each moment take actions that can't
be thwarted.*

"Choiceless" is an invented word because there are no words to contain this principle. Choiceless is founded on two facts: (1) in every activity or process there are certain possibilities that are unavailable in each moment and (2) choices must be made and when they are, there is no choice about what must happen. Again, refer to the chair demonstration.

You can see that at the moment of intent to sit, the volunteer has no choice but to sit. If you expand this example, you can see that there are many moments without choice.

As other examples: the elbow only bends one way; when you pick a foot up and take a step it must come down; if you have a thought it is that thought and not another; when you interpret a circumstance to be good or bad it will be seen as good or bad; and so on. Everything you do, every activity that takes place, has many elements that must occur, because they are needed at specific times throughout an unfolding process for that activity to occur. And wherever a choice can be made, once made, and as long as it is made, there is no choice but to do that.

You might be wondering how this applies to an interaction. The application of the choiceless principle requires that you recognize the many elements about which you or another have no choice but to engage in each moment of an interaction. As you make these distinctions within this principle, you take actions that another or a situation cannot thwart and that cannot be acted on in ways contrary to your actions and objectives. You take advantage of the moment or act for which there is no choice on the other side, turn the activity to your own ends, and accomplish your goals within this space.

For most people, such a relationship is usually much harder to understand than a simpler principle like yielding or following. The first thing that has to happen is to grasp and recognize what no-choice means. As with most effective relating, timing is critical. In one moment, there is no choice about this or that, but that can instantly change in the next moment—making something that wasn't possible a moment ago now possible.

For example, when someone has no intent to take a specific action, they cannot take that action; there is no choice in the matter because intent to act is necessary to act. This intent can be created in a split second, however, so in the next instant they may well be able to act. If you recognize a lack of intent on their part to do a specific act, you are safe to act in relation to the fact that they cannot take action in that moment. The instant their intent changes, however, you must also change your relationship to include the possibility that they can now take that action. At this point you'd switch to focus on some other aspect of which they have no choice. So, obviously, you have to stay up to date and on top of the unfolding processes and match your actions to them continuously and appropriately—and in some fields very quickly—in order to align with the principle.

Can you see how you could apply this principle to your endeavor? It will probably take some serious contemplation and existential thinking to breach the wall of overlooked realities to understand this principle. Once done, you still have to create ways in which you can use this understanding to abide in the principle. It really does work, so see if you can work it out. When you can act in domains that most people can't access or understand, you have a great advantage.

Changing

Allow no effective strategy to be formed
against you.

The last contribution here is a principle you may well not need, but one that presents an interesting exercise in any case. "Changing" as a principle obviously involves changing. But how can change be used as an effective interactive principle? Change always occurs, and in this case, it isn't the fact of change that makes the principle, but your relationship to it.

Any interaction requires change, and to be effective the change needs to be appropriate. Decisions are made in relation to what's perceived, what patterns are recognized, and what extrapolations are imagined. This principle focuses on the fact that others analyze your actions. If they can't get a read on what you're up to, or where you're going, they can't formulate an effective strategy to defeat or manage you. Therefore, you change so fast and so continuously as to make it impossible for another to recognize patterns.

Here, the moment you can discern a plan for your own actions or a method to proceed, change it. You immediately change your plan to something else, something that is not what you are doing now or plan to do. If you can then recognize a new plan or pattern, change again. In this way, anyone relating to your actions will be baffled and unable to take effective action. If you don't know what you're going to do from moment to moment, how could anyone else?

Although you are changing rapidly and in an unprecedented way, you still find your way to a result. The pathway is simply unknown until the very end. It may be like climbing a mountain where you zig and zag, go down as well as up, or dig a tunnel, or fly, or do whatever else is necessary, but eventually find yourself on top of the mountain. An unusual principle, isn't it? If your endeavor doesn't involve interaction between people, this principle may not apply—but if it does, how can you apply it?

A WORLD OF OPERATING PRINCIPLES

As you move through these principles, you will start to glean a few threads that connect them all. Some are more easily seen as related, but all contain the elements of demanding unwavering attention focused on the moment-to-moment unfolding of circumstance and having a specific relationship to circumstances as dictated by the principle. They all also put you in a sophisticated and responsive relationship to what's occurring, easily providing advantageous positioning. From there, mastery is a small step to take.

Certainly, all of these principles are far more than you need. In the martial field, most arts don't know of or use any of them, and those few that do, use only one for their entire art. Even then, it is often not really understood or is used in a limited way. When I would use these principles in fighting, the vast majority of the time any one of them worked on my opponent. Every once in a while, I'd find an opponent against whom one principle wasn't working as well as it should because of the distinctions my opponent was making. So I'd switch to another principle and win.

Over my many decades of fighting, not once did anyone follow me through just one change. If, for example, leading wasn't doing the job as it should—because the opponent's desire wasn't to hit me but to just throw punches, and so he wasn't relating to my movement but only to a stationary target (that wasn't stationary)—I might switch to following and win. Not once did anyone recognize that I changed my principle of operation, and therefore changed their actions accordingly. Even if they had, I had a dozen principles I could use, but I almost never needed to use more than one, and I never needed more than two.

In your case, you'll probably find one or two that best suit your endeavor. But it's educational and enlightening, not to mention fun, to work out each one of them. I recommend, however, to use only one principle at a time throughout a specific interaction. Only if you've mastered more than one and can easily access them in an instant should you attempt to switch principles mid-stream. Even then, once switching, you must stick to the principle constantly throughout the period of time you are engaging that principle.

Conclusion

CUTTING UP AN OX

One of Chuang Tzu's ancient stories points to some of the principles and certainly the sensibilities involved in our search for mastery and effortless effectiveness. The following poetic rendering as gathered by Thomas Merton in his book *The Way of Chuang Tzu** speaks to mastery.

> *Prince Wen Hui's cook*
> *Was cutting up an ox.*
> *Out went a hand,*
> *Down went a shoulder,*
> *He planted a foot,*
> *He pressed with a knee,*
> *The ox fell apart*
> *With a whisper.*
> *The bright clever murmured*
> *Like a gentle wind.*
> *Rhythm! Timing!*

---

*"Cutting Up an Ox" by Thomas Merton, from *The Way of Chuang Tzu*, copyright © 1965 by the Abbey of Gethsemani. Reprinted by permission of New Directions Publishing Corp.

Like a sacred dance,
Like "The Mulberry Grove,"
Like ancient harmonies!

"Good work!" the prince exclaimed,

"Your method is faultless!"
"Method?" said the cook
Laying aside his cleaver,
"What I follow is Tao,
Beyond all methods!

"When I first began
To cut up oxen
I would see before me
The whole ox
All in one mass.

"After three years
I no longer saw this mass.
I saw the distinctions.

"But now, I see nothing
With the eye. My whole being
Apprehends.
My senses are idle. The spirit
Free to work without plan,
Follows its own instinct
Guided by natural line,
By the secret opening, the hidden space,
My clever finds its own way.
I cut through no joint, chop no bone.

"A good cook needs a new chopper
Once a year—he cuts.
A poor cook needs a new one
Every month—he hacks!

"I have used this same cleaver
Nineteen years.
It has cut up
A thousand oxen.
Its edge is as keen
As if newly sharpened.

"There are spaces in the joints;
The blade is thin and keen:
When this thinness
Finds that space

"There is all the room you need!
It goes like a breeze!
Hence I have this cleaver nineteen years
As if newly sharpened!

"True, there are sometimes
Tough joints. I feel them coming,
I slow down, I watch closely,
Hold back, barely move the blade,
And whump! the part falls away
Landing like a clod of earth.

"Then I withdraw the blade,
I stand still
And let the joy of the work

Sink in.
I clean the blade
And put it away."

Prince Wan Hui said,
"This is it! My cook has shown me
How I ought to live
My own life!"

"Cutting Up An Ox" gives a beautiful sense of what it might be like to be a master. Of course, what is missing is the amount of work it took for him to get there. Yet the joy mastery brings to even such simple work shows it provides a life experience that's worth attaining. The journey itself should be a life-changing experience. Although there is a lot of work involved, it can be fun and deeply satisfying.

As I said, this book contains a lot of material, doesn't it? I understand that much of it won't be understood at first. It will take a strong will, lots of contemplation, investigation, experimentation, training, and more to get it all. As you begin to grasp and experience each point in the book, you will still have to take it into action and apply it to mastering your field. Sounds like a huge job, doesn't it?

Remember, this is about you attaining mastery. Perhaps the reason so few people master anything is because of the work and challenges involved. But if you are excited about the adventure, even the work can be fun. Also, you will learn far more than you imagine and undergo an exciting transformation—and the best part is that it will be real and not just a fantasy. Study the material, apply it to your field, and have fun!

The Art of War

By Peter Ralston

Since I was a child I have never lost a war game—those board games in which you fight old battles or wars, such as Gettysburg or D-Day—and I even won my first game when my older brother taught me how to play. Since I was a young adult I never lost a fight, a match, or a tournament in any martial art. To be clear, I'm not saying I'm perfect—I did have troubles on occasion, and sometimes got hit or thrown—but I always prevailed and in the end won the encounter. In 1978, I was the first non-Asian to win a gold medal at the full-contact World Tournament in China. So perhaps I'm qualified to share some understanding of the nature of combat or fighting.

Certain "combative" relationships are actually very common to all humans worldwide. Yet they most often take overlooked forms in our everyday encounters. These are found in such domains as social interactions, business dealings, intimate relationships, community affairs, family gatherings, emotional jousting, mental machinations, and so on. The same principles occur whether speaking about winning a school debate, fighting in a ring, or playing on a field.

Let's be clear, however: we often engage in conflict inappropriately. Many forms of relationship should not be ones of conflict—such as family, marriage, or other forms of partnership. Yet we must confess that even these can turn into warring relationships, at least sometimes. Recognizing what is and isn't competition helps us discover the more hidden or automatic struggles we engage inappropriately and so empowers the possibility of shifting to working together rather than warring in our interactions.

In those interactions where "war" is appropriate—every form of game or sport, self-defense, actual war, business, debate, and so on— then it is good to understand the principles and mind states that help make one successful in these endeavors.

In this segment, I will share a small work that is my version of *The Art of War*. Of course, Sun Tzu's *Art of War* can never be paralleled and certainly not bested. It will always be the original *Art of War*. His writings are about actual wars, one country against another, whereas I'm focused primarily on individual martial interaction, one person against another.

Not very many people are fighters, and far fewer still are master fighters. It is actually a rare achievement. One reason it's rare is because it takes so much training and commitment to accomplish. But even that isn't enough. It also takes intelligence, unusually sensitive perceptions, physical skills, strategic skills, and a host of fine distinctions brought about only through experience and hard-earned insights. If you are interested in fighting skill, I hope this *Art of War* contributes a valuable step toward your own mastery. Since I'm now an old man, I have no more ambitions about participating in combat. Therefore, I find no need to hold back, and so I will share fully what I've learned from a lifetime of successful combat and through insightfully exploring strategic relations.

I give you this advice in simple form, but the experience inside of the advice won't necessarily be easy to access or fully understand. Repeated contemplation, lots of practice, and investigation, observation, and trial and error will be necessary. These nuggets of fighting wisdom give you directions in which to look. Many may seem rather obvious, but you will find they are harder to do than to read about. Once you can shift to actually experiencing and doing what is mentioned, you will realize the reality of it is vastly different from the idea of it. Good luck and happy training.

Ralston's *Art of War*

This rendition of *The Art of War* was written for those in the fighting arena, but the principles, attitudes, and advice may well be applicable to other fields as well.

I. *Attention*
The first thing to do in combat is pay attention!

You must develop the ability to know and to feel where your opponent is and what he is doing in every moment. Never break off from this perception; include everything he does and discern what he is thinking.

Increase your perceptive sensitivity to a high level so that you can "feel" the opponent at all times.*

II. *Feeling-Intelligence*
Let your opponent's actions be felt by you like a wave or wind that pushes up against you—even though there is no physical contact—and let this feeling move your body faster than you can think.

The intelligence you use at this speed can't be funneled through your intellect—which is way too slow. Instead, your actions in response to

---

*When I was a young man, I taught for a time at the San Francisco Olympic Club. One day a year they held Gentleman Jim Corbett's Day in honor of the second man to become a world champion boxer. On this day, in the center of a vast ballroom, a ring was set up and food and drink were served. I was invited to attend because I was teaching children there at the time. I sat at a table with a bunch of "fat cats" smoking cigars and watching the fights. After the first round the men at the table would bet large amounts of money on the fight, choosing one fighter to win. In each case, they chose the fighter that appeared more aggressive and energetic. I could have made a lot of money if I wasn't so poor then, for in each case I chose the other fighter. My choice was based on who was paying attention the most, maintaining a feeling sense of his opponent. And in each case my choice won.

their actions must be immediate and appropriate, and this demands using another kind of intelligence.

Use a feeling-intelligence that has been fine-tuned through lots of study and training so as to know what is advantageous and what is disadvantageous. Get your mind out of the way and respond as a reflection of the opponent's occurring action.

III. Connection
There should be no separation between your opponent's actions and your responses. Your responses should have already happened when your opponent moves—*like a moonbeam that enters as soon as the door is opened.*

Be responsive to everything your opponent does—not in any way reactive, but calm, sensitive, and aware. Always be in charge of your actions, making them advantageous and appropriate without a break or disconnection.

IV. Mind
Keep a calm and present mind. Never let your opponent overwhelm you mentally. If it seems like this may happen, simply refuse delivery.

Keep your mind like steel; let nothing distract or frighten you.

Don't let your own ambitions, plans, fears, distractions, or anything else pull you from a feeling-connection of what the opponent is doing in *every* moment.

Keep your mind open and attention focused.

Don't allow the opponent to control you mentally or emotionally. Neither their determination, anger, ferocity, aggressiveness, nor strength should disturb or bother you or make you hesitant, nor should their fears or weaknesses.

Don't be arrogant, don't be stupid, but don't back down or give up.

Don't get sucked into trying to beat up the opponent. Let the principles dictate what's needed and what actions to take. You serve as a slave to these principles; make haste to follow their commands.

Be committed to the fight. Don't be concerned about surviving it, simply do what is necessary in each moment to win and keep winning. Don't stop until the fight is over.

If you want to fight, don't be an idiot.

V. Body
Stay in touch with your center as a matter of habit.

In combat being centered—feeling and operating from the center of your body, and having your mind "sit" in this place—helps you remain grounded, calm, and powerful. Always use your center and the whole body when you act.

Keep your body relaxed, connected as one whole, grounded, and centered.

Train your body to act immediately as soon as you dictate action. Always be freely balanced and spatially aware. Master your body inside and out so you can act effectively.

VI. Yielding

The best—but not the only—strategy is to never let your opponent use his force against you while you attack with overwhelming odds.

When dealing with force, be like air so your opponent can't find a purchase to use against you. In this way you can remain free and balanced and can take any action needed; you are able to change easily and repeatedly.

Yielding isn't just used to neutralize the opponent's force—it should also be used intelligently to lead or cut his force and take control of his actions.

VII. The Opponent

Have an attitude like you are playing with a child. With a dispassionate and detached mind, always remain mentally superior to your opponent. He should feel as if you are too intelligent, too powerful, and able to change too quickly for him to handle, yet you can handle him easily. But make this real; don't just pretend.

Fighting is fast problem-solving. You have no time to mull things over; you need to see through the opponent's strategy as it relates to what's occurring and immediately change the relationship so that *he* is having a problem, and not you.

Sometimes an opponent offers great challenges. Rise to the occasion. There is always a way to beat someone. Find it!

The opponent is never wrong! It's your job is to relate effectively to whatever is there.

Be intelligent in your fighting. Grasp how the opponent thinks, and interact in a domain outside of his ability to comprehend.

Remember, your opponent is concerned with his own vulnerabilities and ambitions; use these against him. Force him to react to potential exploitation of his vulnerabilities, whether real or not, and keep him off-balance and engaging in defensive activities. Tempt and lead him by presenting apparent vulnerabilities in you that fit with his strategic objectives.

VIII. Change

Your ability to change, even mid-stream, is essential. You should understand and master physical change, strategic change, and emotional and mental change. You even need to change your operating principle when necessary or appropriate.

Change faster than either you or he can think. Be able to move quickly and change rapidly.

IX. Listening

You should be able to read your opponent, but your opponent should only be able to read what you want him to.

Your ability to handle an opponent depends largely on your ability to read his mind and intent. By keeping an ongoing feeling-connection to his every move, you establish constant feedback about his mind, his strategic plans, and his level of intelligence, because his body is always acting under the command of his mind.

Pay attention to your opponent's demeanor—his eyes, his facial expressions, his movements and actions, and his responses and reactions to your movements. From these, use your feeling-intelligence to intuit his mind and outlook, including what he perceives and what he doesn't perceive. Then you will know what to present and what to hide, what strategies to undertake and when to change.

X. Undetectable

Stay calm and relaxed when you attack so that your opponent is hard-pressed to know that's what you're doing. Make your attacks seamless with your other movements so that they don't stand out and are hard to detect.

XI. Advantage

Constantly put and keep your opponent at a disadvantage while you maintain the advantage. If you sense a disadvantage coming up, get the hell out of there—in other words, adjust your position so that the potential disadvantage is nullified.

As the I Ching says: "when in danger, move!"

Keep your opponent at a disadvantage in little things. Adjust your distance, footwork, angles of attack, placement, timing, and all other actions to constantly keep him off-balance, in disarray, having to react defensively, and diminished in power.

XII. Skills

Maneuverability, intelligence, and skill are most important for winning, but power is also necessary.

Skill can always beat brute force. Grace and balance accompany skill.

Develop powers, both physical and mental, that work in combat.

Join your opponent's force and use it for your own ends.

XIII. Beyond Social

You need to understand and transcend cruelty so that you can access what it takes to destroy someone without hesitation. Social conventions have no place in combat; neither social kindness nor social evils should be any part of your state of mind. You should be free to interact in the blink of an eye without the burden of social filters or concerns.

Unnerve your opponent by showing no emotion, only an intense and unflappable intent.

If you're not up for taking advantage of and destroying another, don't fight; perhaps take up piano instead.

XIV. Power

An effortless power is the best power to use. With it you stay balanced, relaxed, and can move and change much more rapidly than you can through brute strength.

Sometimes you need to "blast" your opponent, so you need to have developed the power to do so. To blast your opponent, you act very quickly and with sudden power to knock an opponent off his feet while he is stuck in resistance or defensiveness and is thus unable to mount an effective defense. This option is rarely used, and you should choose wisely when to apply it. If you try and fail, it will reduce your chances of being able to use it in the future, and it will enable and encourage your opponent. Know when it will work and when it won't. Act with decisiveness and without hesitation—and do not fail. It is like cutting through a branch with a sword, you must do it in one stroke and must come out the other side, or you will get stuck inside the branch. See the opportunity arising in a flash and use the center, the ground, and your whole body to cut through what's there.

XV. A Poem

Don't get excited when you see your chance to win.
Stay calm and grounded,
And allow the outcome to occur naturally.

Don't be afraid when they attack with force.
Stay calm and relaxed,
And let their defeat unfold of its own accord.

XVI. Strategy

Use one or more of the effective operating principles (*Huan Sheng*) as a continuous context for your actions.

Huan Sheng: "To spring up on every side, as prolific as thought."
I chose this phrase to represent the pinnacle of my work in effective martial interaction. It embraces the highest and most effective principles that constitute skillful interaction. I have about twelve distinct "arts" or principles in Huan Sheng.

They are all based on the principle of effective interaction: *Your actions must be appropriately related to the occurring event.* Each Huan Sheng is a method or governing principle that creates magical levels of skill and mastery. Here I will simply communicate the essential nature and ingredients that make these methods so powerful; you'll have to contemplate and experiment to work out the reality for yourself.

You should know that these principles and skills are rare and if any one of them were known by some art, it generally would be kept secret and given only to advanced students. Most martial arts have none of these, and no art, except Cheng Hsin, has more than one or two of them. Even in Cheng Hsin, few students have managed to be exposed to all of them. It is important to do these principles justice and to adopt a proper and respectful relationship to them.

Great Operating Principles (Huan Sheng)

Complementing: Mold your actions around your opponent's to fill in where they are not, and empty where they are. Complement their actions like fitting one piece of a puzzle to another; take actions and shapes that complement their actions and shapes as they unfold. Complement their action with yours at the same time as their action, not after. Match and complement their actions, shape, mind, emotions, and strategy.

Following: Follow everything your opponent does, literally. Respond and move along with their actions and mind; stick and yield with or without touch so that you're always in sync and involved with their actions. They direct the action; you follow and keep an advantageous position.

Joining: Merge with your opponent. The first thing to do is sacrifice your will and do their actions along with them, then contribute your actions to theirs, and redirect the whole.

Blending: Join with and become one with whatever your opponent does. While your actions follow theirs, get "inside" their movement by blending your actions with theirs—become one mush of action. Press your feeling-energy into their force so that you feel like you are inside their body and joined with them. Then take over.

Contributing: Do your opponent more than they do. Contribute to what they are doing in such a way that it turns their action and force to their detriment.

Central Joining: Connect with your opponent and move your center to the center of the relationship so that they are forced to move more than you are, and are caught in your orbit—like swinging a rock on a string, where the rock moves faster and far more than your hand. When your opponent has to make more movement than you in the same period of time, you can take over because they are controlled by your center and action. Don't engage in centrifugal force. Instead, always bring them spiraling into you so that you can keep control.

Integral Joining: Connect your actions to your opponent's whole body all at once so that when you move one inch their whole body is moved at the same time.

Leading: Know that you are a target. Offer opportunities and move the target to control their actions. You must follow (their intent, desire, perspective, and strategy) in order to lead. Want them to attack you, present "attractive" opportunities to them. Move at the beginning of or before their action to force them to change the direction of their actions, and so control them. Then once they have committed to the change, nearer to the end of that action, change to your advantage. Timing is important.

For example, you can lead your opponent to attack to the left by moving left and then changing to the right suddenly when they commit to the left, attacking them in that moment. Or, you can draw them out of their power base, tempting them by being vulnerable, but a bit farther than is good for them, making them more vulnerable as they extend out to try to take advantage of you. Or, you can lead them astray by taking actions that suggest an outcome, thus getting them to take the action you want. Or, you can lead them to collide with their own actions by drawing them out and leading them back into themselves.

Cutting: Reduce or eliminate your opponent's potential for effective action, power, intent, or perception by moving your body to a place that reduces their power and potential given their immediate structure and objective. Move to reduce or destroy the effectiveness of their action *before* they make it by perceiving what they intend to do or what they *can* do and are likely to do. Adjust your position where you can still engage but if they take that action, it will be ineffective or less effective. You either force them to change, but beat them to the punch before they can manage, or take advantage of them if they attempt the action. As with all such principles, make this activity constant, not a technique.

Borrowing: Learn to fold around your opponent's actions so if they block you in any way you're like water that goes around and through—that's called folding. Then learn to borrow their force to use it for your own ends, cycling or springing it back on them. Let them do the work. Borrow but give back. You must stay relaxed, open the major joints, and use intrinsic strength to "catch" their force, by channeling it into the ground, using their force to compress your body and cycle it back.

Even More Advanced Operating Principles

Sprouting: Not falling behind. Handle whatever the opponent intends to do before they begin any movement and before you're required to take action. Be in the "before" place by perceiving their intent before physical action can take place, or at least in the very beginning of the action—the preparative adjustment of the body that readies it to take action—and nip it in the bud. Do this by taking action before they do, destroying their potential action with your own action.

Changing: Change into what is appropriate in relationship to them *now*—what is most immediate, before even you can interpret it. Stay with what is becoming and change so rapidly that even you don't know what's next. Change just to change; if you know what you're going to do next, then do something else. This way your opponent can't formulate an effective strategy. While you change at great speed, take advantage of their confusion.

Choiceless: Use the fact that choosing (to act, interpret, place attention, and so on) means that your opponent has no choice; they cannot do other than what they are doing. Perceive what they can and can't do in each moment and relate to them by maneuvering and taking action so that they have no choice in the matter. If they do, you have fallen behind. Stay on top of the relationship so that you are always relating to what they have no choice about, and defeat them. This also occurs with high-speed adjustments and fast changes.

Meta-Advanced Operating Principles

Completion (Timeless): Already done. Will that the beginning and the end occur in the same moment and place; the beginning is already ending. It's like creating a time warp where you eliminate intermediate process and create a fusion between the beginning and the result so that it all seems to occur in the blink of an eye. As soon as you begin you are finishing.

Inclusion (Heaven and Earth): Be all-inclusive, encompass all that is occurring (in process) so that the outcome is inevitable; make your mind and energy so big there is no outside; be beyond connected. In this place, stitch everything together so that there is no possibility of conflict or discord; all activity is resolved before opposition can arise.

Ox Cutting: Find the spaces of no resistance. Discern where your opponent cannot resist or thwart or even neutralize, and enter. Stay in this place until the job is done.

The fundamental shift for being effective in fighting is a complete and present acceptance, feeling, and joining of the opponent (inside and out). Accept, feel, and join them in whatever action they are doing or disposition they have. This does not mean you lose yourself; it simply means that your experience and actions are always related to theirs, and you experientially include them "as they are" without resistance or ignorance.

The Prime Principle: Remember, what all these principles have in common is that they demand keeping your attention on your opponent in every moment in order to know what to do, and just as constantly responding to *everything* they do, no matter how small or apparently insignificant it is. This creates a constant and ongoing effective relating to each moment.

Index

About the Author

In 1975 Peter Ralston founded the Cheng Hsin School, and in 1977 he opened a center called the Cheng Hsin School of Internal Martial Arts and Center for Ontological Research in Oakland, California. In 1978 he became the first non-Asian to win the full-contact martial World Championship held in China. In both mind work and martial arts, his approach has always been to lead students away from what is merely believed and toward a powerful personal experience of discovering for themselves what is true.

He is the creator of the Art of Effortless Power—a large-scope internal martial art focused on being effortlessly effective—as well as Empowerment, his own genre of Consciousness work, assisting people to investigate and contemplate what's true about being and reality.

Ralston is the author of several books, including *The Principles of Effortless Power, Zen Body-Being,* and his powerful trilogy, *The Book of Not Knowing, Pursuing Consciousness,* and *The Genius of Being.*

His website is PeterRalston.com.